TABLE OF CONTENTS

DEDICATION

To Carl

INTRODUCTION

After the success of my previous book, The Tidy Closet, readers asked me if I could do the same for the kitchen. I thought about it. There was obviously a demand for such a book, so the answer was of course, yes! However, that wasn't the only reason for writing the book you now hold in your hands.

The second reason was a personal one. My kitchen is a joy to me. It's a place where I can relax, prepare simple food and express myself through cooking, for my family and friends. I feel that cooking is an act of love and sharing born within me from my early years growing up in France. 'Les plaisirs de la table' (pleasures of the table) is a very important concept pour les Français. I want you to experience the same love and joy in your kitchen, if not for your family then for yourself.

The kitchen is the heart of the home. It should be the place where health is maximised and stress minimised. Good food doesn't have to take much time to prepare. It can be faster than going out to buy a ready made meal. But, it can take longer if your kitchen is not tidy and organised.

By tidying and organising your kitchen, you may find that you have time to cook after all. You have the ingredients necessary, the kitchen is clean and you can reach the sink. You eat well and more healthily. You look and feel better. Your confidence soars. People notice a change in you. You are more alive and more fun to be with. If you cook for your family, they may begin to spend more time at the table instead of shut away in different rooms. Meal times may be had around the dining table. As a result, you may feel closer as a family unit.

To let you know what you're in for, I set out below a brief synopsis of each chapter.

Chapter 1 Clutter 101
Right from the off, I will show you the difference between being a clutterer and a hoarder. I will set out the reasons you may clutter and the excuses you might make for why you don't tidy after yourself, or anyone else for that matter. We get straight into some exercises to help you on your way.

Chapter 2 You Are Here

To move forward, you need to know where you are, so we discuss your current situation. As you may be lacking organisational know-how and motivation, we have to change the way you think. This is a book for active participation. It isn't for the faint at heart.

Chapter 3 Disadvantages And Benefits
Chapter 3 sets out the numerous disadvantages of clutter and disorganisation and points out the many benefits of a tidy kitchen. You'll be given very clear ideas about why a tidy and well organised kitchen isn't just a luxury but a necessity.

Chapter 4 Motivation
In this chapter, you'll get many practical tools to help you start the decluttering process. Getting charged up for success is a vital step, not just in the kitchen but in all areas of your life.

Chapter 5 Planning
Chapters 5, 6 and 7 are the heart of this book. In Chapter 5, we'll get down to the nitty gritty and formulate your campaign to declutter and organise your kitchen.

Chapter 6 How To Tidy And Clean By Area
Learn how to declutter and organise each area of the kitchen, from appliances to units and shelving, even crockery. All you need is here!

Chapter 7 D-Day
This is it! The day you (and your kitchen) have been waiting for. Using all that you've read and learned, you'll put your campaign into effect. The Tidy Kitchen awaits.

Chapter 8 Organisation
This chapter will give you ideas and advice on how to organise your kitchen so that it becomes a space that works for you, not the other way around: Zen in the art of kitchen maintenance!

Chapter 9 Keep It all Going
Finally, you will get help, advice and tips on how you can maintain a tidy kitchen, whether you have a few minutes to spare or a few hours. You may have had to wrestle your kitchen into shape but keeping it that way doesn't have to be a fight. Relax into your dream kitchen and live the life of a

culinary queen.

Tips and exercises are peppered throughout the book to give you additional help, food for thought and ideas to digest. Get a little notebook so you can keep all of your notes together in one place. It will be important to jot down your thoughts and ideas as they occur whilst doing the exercises. Some of the realisations that you make about yourself may be important life lessons.

If you follow this book carefully and do what I suggest, I guarantee that your kitchen will look better, even if only a little.

I hope you will enjoy The Tidy Kitchen and will take from it one thing, or many things, that will instil in you that very French feeling of 'Les plaisirs de la table' in your very own tidy kitchen.

So, let's go to it; Tidy Kitchen, here we come. 'Allons-y!'

CHAPTER 1
Clutter 101

The Difference Between A Clutterer And A Hoarder

For those of you who've read my previous book The Tidy Closet, you'll already know the difference between a clutterer and a hoarder. Readers who haven't yet read it may be worried about whether they're a hoarding master or simply disorganised. I'll give you a condensed explanation of the difference between the two terms here.

You are a clutterer when:

Your home lacks order.
You misplace items regularly due to chronic disorganisation.
You lack the willingness, motivation or skills to tackle the issue.
You are aware, or admit that, there is a problem.

Take consolation in that one third of the general population is a clutter-bug.

Compared to a clutterer, a hoarder is a very different person.

You are a hoarder when:

You are unaware or unwilling to acknowledge that there is a problem.
Your house may be a health hazard or an accident waiting to happen.
Your house may have to be condemned by the Health and Safety Department due to the dangers to life and limb.
Nobody visits.
Objects, usually collections of the same or similar things, have taken over your house.
Stuff is piled floor to ceiling, in every single cupboard and on every available surface.
There is no space left, but you keep bringing new stuff into your home.
You may have to sleep on the sofa, if it can be found under the mountains of stuff.

Only 1% of the population can be deemed to be hoarders. If you've bought this book and are aware of the situation, or want to change it, you can safely guess that you are simply a clutterer.

If you're worried or have any doubt, a quick chat with your doctor ought to put your mind at rest.

Reasons Why You Are In The Kitchen Clutter Club

Maybe you've never heard of kitchen organisation at all and were not interested until now. Or, your kitchen may have started fairly tidy and organised. Then, life took over. One day, you get hit by the realisation that your kitchen looks like a bomb has hit it. You wonder how it happened. It didn't happen overnight, or maybe it did! In this chapter, we will explore the many reasons and, yes the excuses, why your kitchen is untidy and cluttered.

Understanding the reasons why your kitchen is cluttered will help you address your clutter demons. In this way, once your kitchen is tidy and organised, you'll be less likely to slip back into your old ways.

Consider List

As a first exercise, make a heading in your notebook titled 'Consider List'. This will be an inventory of all things you may want to get rid of. As you think of items in your kitchen that you no longer need or want, add them to this list. We'll revisit this 'Consider List' later. Listing things early on will give you time to mull over whether you want to keep them or ditch them.

Having started your 'Consider List', skip a few pages and make a new heading 'Reasons For Clutter'. Let's explore some of those reasons now.

Procrastination

Good old procrastination could be all that is stopping you from doing any clearing up in your kitchen. Just the thought of housework is enough to make you run a mile. In fact, yes, you'd rather do anything else. You tend to either leave it to the last minute or push it aside and forget it. Procrastinating used to work for you but now the problem has grown too much to ignore.

 Exercise

Consider whether you are a procrastinator. Try to think of examples of how you may avoid tidying the kitchen. We can be very inventive when we want to avoid doing something!

Lack of Time

A lack of time is often a major reason (some would call it an excuse) for avoiding housework. Although we seem to enjoy more leisure time than ever before, paradoxically we are busier too. Work, children, being the head of the household, full or part-time activities, interests and responsibilities, all eat into our time like never before. As a result, the kitchen gets neglected. Little by little, the cupboards fill up, the fridge gets dirtier, worktops disappear under clutter, grime accumulates on the stove and in the oven. Before you know it, your kitchen is on the way to being a health hazard.

(Please note that in the US 'worktops' are called 'countertops'. Having lived in Europe all my life, I will continue to use 'worktops' throughout this book).

 Exercise

Take a moment now to write down all the reasons why you say you lack the time to keep your kitchen clutter free.

Consider each one and think of ways you may be able to make time to do some kitchen clearing. Don't clutter, clear!

Shopping

Even though you can't find the time to tidy your kitchen, you're able to go shopping for more things. More food, more bits and bobs, the latest celebrity chefs' thing-a-me-jig for doing this, that or the other pack your trolley. Your kitchen fills up weekly, if not daily, but you carry on shopping regardless. Shopping is what you do on a Saturday, on the way home from work or online. It is 'you' time, for zoning out and forgetting all your cares and worries. Your kitchen, however, is showing the strain.

Exercise

Write down all the reasons why you like to shop.

Think about finding alternative ways to get much needed 'you' time without accumulating things. Being tidy and organised is all about doing more with less. By the end of this book, you may find that tidying and organising your kitchen could be the 'you' time you've been looking for.

Bulk Buy

You can't resist a bargain. Who can? This is what those clever sales people know all too well. You are subjected to a barrage of high pressure sales, from dawn to dusk, coercing you to play your part in keeping the wheels of industry turning.

Not only do you buy what you may not need but you end up buying it in bulk! Consider the following: do you really need to buy 10 kgs of flour if you don't bake very often? You may reason that the price per kilo is so much cheaper. However, will you be able to use it all before the dreaded 'Best Before Date' expires? Probably not. You'll have to throw most of it away. Then, off you go to the shops to be enticed by the 'bulk buy baloney' all over again.

✎ Exercise

Make a list of all the things you have in bulk.

Decide now to make a special effort to use them all.

In future, when faced with bulk buy offers, ask yourself the following questions:

Will the foodstuff be consumed before its 'Best Before Date'?
Is this a product my household uses or will use?
Is it too large to store?

Is it junk food?
Is it just junk?

Unused Presents

It's easy to fall into the sentimentality snare. That broken china cup can't be thrown out because it was a gift. The bread-maker that weighs a ton and takes up so much space can't be given away (even though you've baked a loaf only once). It was a wedding present after all. You couldn't possibly part with the large brown Rumtopf you inherited from Aunty Gertrude as it's a purported family heirloom.

It's a fair assumption that you have at least one such sentimental piece lurking in your kitchen right now.

You may feel some guilt at getting rid of these items. However, they've been languishing for a long time, unused and even forgotten. They've been unloved and have gathered dust. Wouldn't you feel better giving them to someone who'd use them? They may benefit that person more than you. So, release yourself from the unhealthy grip of guilt. When I give something like this away, I add a little caveat. Once the receiver tires of it, or no longer has a use for it, he or she should feel free to give it away in their turn. I assure them I won't get upset and that I'd rather something be loved and used than disappear into the back of someone else's cupboard. What do you think?

A little note here. I'm not advocating that you must give away every unused item that has a sentimental attachment. What I'm saying is that you'll come to realise that there is a time for something to go. It may be now. It may be tomorrow, next week or next year. If you really can't part with Aunty Gertrude's Rumtopf right now, keep it. That's perfectly fine. In the end, what you need in your kitchen are things that are useful and/or loved.

✎ Exercise

Add all your unused presents in your kitchen whether it's crockery, china, small electrical appliances, gadget, foodstuff or utensil to your 'Consider List'. Be thorough! This is a very good opportunity to open every cupboard and drawer. Look on every work surface and on top of every unit. Become acquainted with the scale of your problem whilst focusing on this exercise.

Are you sure you've noted everything? If you've skipped an area, please go back and look again. It may be a very hard thing for you to do. You may not want to open some cupboards or drawers. You may know what's in there and dread opening them. Believe me, you have to take ownership of the problem and admit responsibility for it. Once you do, you'll be amazed how much easier this whole task becomes.

Cherished

One step further along the sentimentality trail are things that have sentimental value but have not been given to you. You may have acquired a set of multi-coloured Venetian shot glasses on your travels or have picked up other pieces that are special to you. You may not have any use for them but they are cluttering up your cupboards.

What can be done with these? Just as before, if they give you pleasure when you look at them, keep them. They bring a positive energy to your day. They remind you of a special person, moment or event. However, if you lack space in your kitchen, try to find another place for them.

I can't stress enough that I am not here to brow beat you into giving away all that you love and cherish simply for the utilitarian. This book is here to help you simplify and organise your kitchen around the things that you use and love.

 Exercise

Add to your 'Consider List' all the cherished items in your kitchen.

♥ Tip

Start a treasure chest where some, or all, loved but unused pieces are kept safe and in one place.

Big-Ticket

How many times have you heard the cry "I can't get rid of that! It cost me a fortune"?

We all have items on which we spend an arm and a leg but, once they are in our kitchen, there is little or no use for them. They don't do what they were made for very well, or at all. Even worse, we already had something at the back of a cupboard that did their job just as well, or better. In all this clutter, we had just forgotten we had them! Due to the high price tags, the thought of giving these items away, or selling them for less than we paid, sends shivers down our spines. You are filled with embarrassment for spending so much in the first place. In denial, you persuade yourself to hang on to them and into the back of a cupboard they go.

✎ Exercise

Add your unused big-ticket items to your 'Consider List'.

Unique

You may have a few items that you feel are unique or rare. That Fabergé egg that sits on the shelf above the sink looks pretty, but is it really serving a purpose? I jest of course! The reason these things are cluttering up your kitchen is because you are convinced that they are antique or one of a kind.

✎ Exercise

Again, add these unique pieces to your 'Consider List'.

Ask yourself the following questions.

Is it the uniqueness of these items that makes you keep them?

Are you using them?
Do they enhance your kitchen?
Do you love them?

Reconsider the need to keep them. Maybe they are not as unique as you think. A quick search online may give you the answer or perhaps a quick valuation at a local antique dealer of good repute will shatter your illusion about your Fabergé egg. If it does however turn out to be a real Fabergé egg, well, you can now afford the kitchen of your dreams!

Bric A Brac

Your kitchen may be the repository for everything that doesn't have a place anywhere else in the house. After all, if it doesn't belong in the sitting room, dining room, bedroom, bathroom, garage or garden shed then it has to belong in the kitchen, right?

We all have a drawer, unit or worktop overflowing with paperwork unattended to, magazines (cookery or otherwise), cleaning products, loose recipes, old plastic tubs, baby things, homework, old laptops, matches, elastic bands or phone chargers. The list is endless! They all get dumped in the kitchen because it's the hub of the house or it's the first room people come into. It's easier to dump things there than find a place for them.

✎ Exercise

Write these down on the 'Consider List'. I hope you left enough room!

Alongside each item, write down where or to whom these things really belong. Further on in the book, we'll get to the part about putting stuff away. It may even be that you can present a box of stuff to your house mate, husband or children and say "this is yours, find a place for it out of the kitchen." Reclaim your kitchen as the hub of the home, not the heap of the house.

Having read through this chapter so far, take some time to think about the reasons for clutter that you've written down and the items on your 'Consider List'. Do you see any common themes or patterns? These are your personal clutter demons. Resolve to address each and every one so that they never haunt your kitchen again.

Excuses For Not Tackling The Clutter

You may have a tendency to make excuses for why you haven't tackled the clutter in your kitchen. They are used to deflect responsibility. Below are examples of excuses that might ring bells. Pick and choose the ones that sound the most familiar to you:

No time.
At work all day.
I didn't make the mess.
Why should I be the only one to tidy up?
Not my problem.
I get no help.
I only live here.
Too tired.
Other things to do.
Can't be bothered.
What about my TV program?

✎ Exercise

Can you think of five of your own excuses for not tidying and organising your kitchen? List them below or in your notebook.

Consider these excuses and resolve to never use them for the state of your kitchen again.
Finally, think about whether you are making excuses for other members of the household who contribute to the mess. Are you allowing them to get

away with it? It may be because you don't want to create a fuss or cause an argument. The role of peacekeeper is one of your ever growing list of job titles.

It's time to get tough, not only with yourself but also with the rest of the household. You have to eliminate the reasons and stop the excuses. Accepting full responsibility is one of the first steps towards your tidy and organised kitchen. There can be no long-term solution otherwise.
So, start motivating yourself and others. This book will help you and give you the 'how'.

 Exercise

The final exercise of this chapter is to write out 100 times
'I admit responsibility and I will no longer make excuses' ;0)

In the next chapter we will examine your current situation. Alas, it may not be pretty.

CHAPTER 2
You Are Here

The sheer sight of your cluttered kitchen is probably sapping every ounce of willpower that you have. You want a tidy kitchen but you feel overwhelmed by the scale of the task ahead. You fear that you don't have the time required for such an undertaking. You worry that you'll never get the job done. But, you also get anxious thinking about the wasted food, unsavoury conditions and grime. You may secretly feel so ashamed that you've stopped inviting friends and family around. You may feel guilty that you aren't cooking for your immediate family as much as you feel you should.

These competing feelings are at loggerheads. On the one hand, you feel it's all too much and on the other you feel that you want to, or ought to, do something.

This chapter is all about the situation you're in now. See how much of this is familiar.

You Are Here

Your ideal kitchen, in your mind's eye, is a perfectly planned, organised and clean space where you can prepare and cook the most wonderful meals. It's a kitchen that has everything that you need (note I did not say everything that you want) in the right place and the freshest ingredients stored in the right way. The worktops are clean and clear of clutter. The sink is empty of dishes. The fridge, stove and other appliances gleam and sparkle. This is your destination, your vision of what your ideal kitchen will look like. It may not match what your kitchen looks like right now, but you want it.

Before you can get to where you want to go, it's necessary to know where you are. At the moment, you're lost and confused. What you need to start your journey is a map with a big red arrow labelled 'you are here'.

This chapter is about where you are. Let's take stock.

The fridge is full to the brim of perishing or already perished food. The vegetable drawer can't be opened without a good pull as everything is crammed in tighter than stuffing inside the Christmas turkey. Tomatoes, lettuce, peppers and aubergines are bruised and limp, if not rotten. Soggy potatoes, still in their plastic bag, have sprouted shoots and grown roots. Tubs of mayonnaise, bottles of tomato sauce and jars of mustard have sticky and crusted lids.

Before cooking any meal, the sink has to be cleared of yesterday's or last week's dishes. The stainless steel certainly didn't look this matt in the showroom!

The dishwasher has become an expensive extra cupboard. It's full of clean dishes from the last time it was switched on. Your units are so full you can't fit all the dishes in. You feel that the dishwasher is the best place for them right now. Still, it could be worse. It could be full of smelly dishes that haven't yet been washed!

The worktops are covered with things that nobody knows what to do with. Before preparing any meal, you need to push everything to one side with a swipe of your arm. There is no chance of baking on a whim as you have nowhere to make pastry.

The units are crammed full of dishes, plates and bowls that have never been used.

Drawers are packed with useless bits and pieces. On the few occasions that you manage to ram them closed, they become so jammed that only a few hard yanks will force them open again.

The kitchen table, on which you'd love to serve meals for the entire family, is covered in homework, your husband's (or your) accounts and bank statements. It is a table, desk, office, cupboard, drawer all in one. You eat at one end of the table or in front of the TV with the plate on your knees.

The floor is sticky and the tiles have long lost their shine.

The walls are covered with sticky finger marks and a plethora of notes on yellow Post-Its.

If any, or heaven forbid, all the above describes your kitchen, don't you think it's time to do something? I know it all seems overwhelming but don't worry, help is at hand.

No Motivation

You may have bought this book because you're looking for motivation. You may be desperate to tackle the mess and grime but don't know where to start. Perhaps you just want to scream. Well, who wouldn't? The sheer scale of the task may be too much to contemplate. It's natural to feel deflated and unmotivated when you're faced with a kitchen to die in, rather than to die for.

Just imagine that you've decided to tidy your kitchen but you don't know where to start. Your thinking goes something like this:

You want to wash the dishes and clean the sink but should you empty the dishwasher first? You then realise you have nowhere to put the dishes you'll take out of the dishwasher. You therefore decide to tidy up the table to make room for the dishes. But you have nowhere to put the things that are on the table either. Suddenly, you remember that your best friend is coming around for coffee. You need to clear the table. So you cram everything that's on the table into the dishwasher, close the door and breathe a sigh of relief.

This scenario is a little far fetched, however the point is that all the tasks that need to be done depend on another being completed first. It's enough to make you run for the hills. No wonder you may opt for take away meals so often. You don't need to cook and if you eat straight out of the cartons, there's no washing up. Doesn't that sound much easier? Of course it does.

I shall do my best to give you the motivation you need. There will be more exercises to do and I will share helpful tips and advice. Oh, and about the question of what to do first: here's the thing. It doesn't really matter what you do first. You just have to make a start.

Lacking Organisational Know-How

Not everyone is a born organiser. I'm not. Organising is a skill that I've learned over the years. We all pick up ideas of what to do to make our everyday lives work as we go along. But occasionally, we need a little help and a shove in the right direction.

I will share with you ways to make your kitchen life more organised. After that, only a little time will be needed on a regular basis to keep your kitchen in Homes and Gardens, not Dante's Ninth Circle of Hell.

My regular readers know that I love to simplify everything from style to lifestyle, from cleaning to cooking. Why complicate your life unnecessarily?

I will encourage you every step of the way so that you don't lose momentum or hope. You will get there. Don't worry.

The following chapter sets out the disadvantages of a cluttered kitchen and the benefits of a tidy one. These need to be set out clearly so that you can begin to feel the motivation necessary to change your ways. So, 'en avant!'

CHAPTER 3
Disadvantages And Benefits

The Disadvantages Of Clutter And Disorganisation

Clutter has many disadvantages. Some are aesthetic, some are psychological and some physical. All have an adverse impact on you and your hopes for a tidy kitchen.

Clutter leaves you with less space. You have allowed, willingly or unwittingly, large amounts of stuff to pile up. The result is less room for what is necessary. Removing the superfluous for the essential is a must to ensure that your kitchen becomes clutter-free and well organised. Let's look at some of the disadvantages of clutter now. Pay attention, because at the end of this section, I will ask you to write down how the state of your kitchen affects you. This will give you important information when tackling the clutter in your kitchen.

Jumbled Up

Weeks, months or years of clutter and disorganisation have left the units, worktops and drawers in an awful state. Everything is in a muddle. The more you lift, pull and push the clutter around in an attempt to find something the messier it all gets.

Nothing To Use

Because nothing has been tidied away, you waste time looking for things. As you can't unearth your good plates and glasses, you set out the chipped plates for dinner and drink wine out of the kids' plastic beakers.

Mistreatment

Nothing in your kitchen is loved. Everything gets damaged. Fruit and vegetables get bruised. Foodstuffs have their packets split and have to be thrown out. Crockery and glasses get chipped and cracked. Appliances get damaged, doors and drawers get scuffed, cracked and warped.

Waste of Time and Money

Clutter wastes not only time but also money. You may swear blind you already have something, but as it can't be found, you have to replace it. Food gets damaged and goes rotten before you can eat it, so again you have to buy more. Once you get organised, you'll have an enjoyable working kitchen which will cost you less in terms of money and time to run it. That is something to look forward to, 'non'?

Mismatched

Whilst the shabby chic look is very chic and I am a fan myself, it's good to have sets of things that are complete. You may have started with an idea in mind about the kind of style your kitchen, crockery and utensils should have. Lately, however that has gone awry. You've long forgotten that your main dinner set has red flowers (or dancing jalapeño peppers), or that your utensils should match the ones you already have in stainless steel. When something gets lost or broken you feel you don't have the time to search out the same brand, make or style. You tell yourself it isn't important and buy the first thing that comes to hand. They may even have stopped making your dancing jalapeño pepper dinner service altogether!

Fleeting Trends

One of the disadvantages of clutter is that it promotes a lack of coherent vision. As a result, you fall prey to fleeting culinary fashion trends. Every season seems to bring some new culinary celebrity to the business of cookware and tableware. We are persuaded that cooking or serving our food using X's own brand ware is the answer to all our kitchen woes. Well, believe me, it isn't. It only adds to it. The look lasts one season, perhaps two, then goes out of fashion. You are left with an ever dwindling supply of something that is no longer manufactured.

The same is true for foodstuffs and ingredients. To keep the ever growing culinary industry churning out new things, the men at the top seek out ever more remote cooking flavours, trends and styles. One minute, it's one country's style and flavour that's all the rage. The next, we've jumped to some other culture. For all this, you need new ingredients and cooking gadgets. Your cupboards get stuffed with ever more far flung foodstuffs, none of which can possibly be fresh, having flown half way round the world.

My advice is to find your authentic style; stick with it and let fashion trends come and go. It makes more sense to prepare fresh, local produce that you know about than to keep experimenting with unfamiliar flavours garnered from TV programs or books. Neither can tell you what something tastes like. On the other hand, you already know the flavour of your own style of food. You cook from the heart with confidence and knowledge about its flavour. The result is well prepared, well cooked and well flavoured food. I am not saying 'don't experiment'. Experimentation is a cook's raison d'être. I am saying 'do not follow things on a whim: stay true to yourself'.

Exile

The kitchen, once your pride and joy and the focus of your home, is now a place where you fear to tread. You feel exiled. You go there reluctantly, with a heavy heart and feelings of woe. It's no wonder that your cooking may look and taste uninspired. The more often plates come back to the kitchen with half-eaten food the worse you feel. It's high time to reclaim your kitchen.

Frustration

It's no surprise that the state of your kitchen and your inability to use it to its full potential leaves you frustrated. I will motivate you to tidy and organise your kitchen. By decluttering, you will rediscover your culinary roots and style. The decision about what to serve and how to serve it will become apparent to you.

Clothing and cooking to my mind are very similar. Strip away all that is not you, deduct all that is fancy and frivolous, remove what others are trying to foist upon you and you will find the real you. I assure you that the heart of your kitchen is still under the clutter somewhere.

Stress

Frustration and annoyance leave you stressed. As we all know, stress is bad for you. It causes all manner of physical and emotional problems. Clutter and disorganisation will contribute to ill health. Do not underestimate this. Clutter assaults the senses until you want to scream, run, cry or all three at the same time. I bet my next meringue that you can do without the additional stress of an untidy and disorganised kitchen. Together, let's turn your kitchen back into the haven of peace that it should be.

 Exercise

I hope that you've been paying attention through all the above as it's time to do an exercise. Write down all the disadvantages of your cluttered kitchen and how they affect you. You can add to the list as you go through the book. The more you understand how the clutter is affecting you the more powerful your motivation to change will become.

You may be surprised at how far the tentacles of clutter and disorganisation reach into your life.

For example:

You didn't have an ingredient for a dish you wanted to prepare so had cornflakes instead.
You were unable to find something, got frustrated and shouted at the kids.
The wonky timer on the oven burned the roast for an important dinner party.
You pulled out the wrong plug from the wall socket when you went on holiday and the freezer defrosted.

The Benefits Of A Tidy Kitchen

Now let's explore the benefits of a tidy, simple and well organised kitchen. You'll see that there are many. As above, we'll end with an exercise. This time, you'll be asked to list the benefits that you feel a tidy and well organised kitchen will bring to you and the positive ways they will affect your life. Once you've realised the positive changes that these benefits can bring, you'll be keen to get going and reluctant to slip back into your old ways.

Focus

With cluttered surfaces and overflowing units, it's impossible to focus your eyes, let alone your mind, on anything but the mess. Everything competes for attention. Not only aesthetically, but also practically, your eyes have difficulty in settling on one item. Once surfaces are clear and you're confident that the units will not burst open at any minute, you'll achieve a clarity of focus. Whether it's preparing the next meal, some spur of the moment baking or just flicking through your favourite cook books, everything will be easier.

Calm

You've probably heard of the expression 'calm before the storm'. Well, every kitchen has its frantic moments, such as in the middle of cooking that next 'wow' meal. However, both before and after, it should be calm and serene; ready at a moment's notice for culinary magic to happen.

When a kitchen isn't in good shape, even simple, mundane tasks take an almost Herculean effort to carry out. This adds strain to your already stressful life. After a long exhausting day, you wish for a relaxing time at home. Decluttering your kitchen is one of the many steps you can take towards attaining more calm. The kitchen is probably the place where busy cooks spend most of their home time. So, it makes sense to whip it into shape sooner rather than later. Who knows? Once started, the decluttering and organising may creep along the corridor into the sitting room, from there, up the stairs into the bedrooms and bathrooms. Once you've caught the bug, you may not be able to stop.

Precious Time

We all suffer from lack of time in our lives. If you say you haven't got the time to clear and tidy your kitchen, consider the following. Assume it takes a day, i.e. eight hours of uninterrupted effort, to get your kitchen licked into shape.

How long do you spend looking for things in the kitchen over the course of a year?
How often do you go to the shops and buy something you already have at the back of a drawer?
How many more examples can you think of?
How much time do you spend wishing you had a tidier kitchen?

When you think like this, the issue becomes not whether you do or don't have the time to tidy your kitchen, but whether you can afford the time not to!

In The Tidy Closet, I set out a very important concept about time or the lack of it. It's called the principle of the irreducible minimum. Can you spare a minute right now to tidy some part of your kitchen? No one can say that they don't have one minute to spare. Try it now. Success? I hope so. If you can spare one minute, believe me you can spare five. If you can spare five, you can spare fifteen. If you can spare a quarter of an hour, why not half an hour and so on? See, all of a sudden your available time seems to expand. Time doesn't change but your perception of its availability does. Once you start thinking like this, your priorities will change to allow you to achieve more.

Once the kitchen is the way you want it, or more appropriately, the way you NEED it, you will no longer waste time. Preparing and cooking food will be done faster, more efficiently and will be more enjoyable. You'll free up your precious time for what's important: you, your family and your friends.

Money

Hands up who doesn't want to save money.
Hands up all those who, seeing three pots of mustard in their pantry, add 'mustard' to their shopping list.
Finally, hands up all those who spend a fortune at the shops, then throw all their shopping into the bin on getting home.
Nobody? Of course not.

A well thought-out shopping list can save you a lot of money. But, in many cases a 'shopping list', if one is written at all, may as well be called a 'shopping lost' for all the money that's wasted.

On sorting out your cupboards, you'll find many duplicates, items out of date and others you bought thinking you'd use them but didn't. This will soon be a thing of the past. As you and your kitchen get organised, you'll have a proper 'list', not a 'lost'. You'll only shop for things that you need. No more wasting your hard earned cash. Your money will be in your account and not in the quarterly earnings reports of the big supermarket companies. Be quids in, not quids out.

Less Is More

More is not always more. Countless gadgets, accessories, ingredients and enough china to serve 200 guests are not the recipe for better meals. Do more with less.

Having fewer ingredients makes you use your imagination, try out new recipes and new combinations. Having fewer gadgets and accessories leaves you more time to cook. Less time is spent looking around finding them, remembering how to use them and cleaning them afterwards. Having less china won't make your food less tasty. Try it out for yourself. Keep a log of every time you use a gadget or set of china.

Keep in mind that for something to be useful, it must be used. If it isn't used, it has no use. If you don't use it, lose it.

Tidy And Happy

Enormous pleasure is to be had from a job well done. Cleaning and tidying the kitchen will be no different. There might, and probably will, be sweat and tears in the doing. However, in the sitting back and looking at what you've achieved, there will be a sense of pride and fulfilment. Simply doing it to make you feel good is reason enough. Mountains are there to be climbed and deserts are there to be crossed. You may not be a mountaineer or Lawrence of Arabia but you can be a kitchen conqueror.

Saving Space

When cupboards are crammed so tight you can't squeeze a bay leaf in edgeways, you know things are not right. On the contrary, who isn't amazed at the things that can be fitted into tiny spaces when done tidily?

Taking everything out of the cupboards and putting it all back in neatly allows you to fit so much more in. Consider this first if you are thinking of redesigning your kitchen due to lack of room. You may save yourself thousands of pounds or dollars. Reclaim the space you thought was lacking but which may already be in your kitchen; use it, don't abuse it.

Energy Flow

Chinese Medicine says that energy (chi) flows freely around a healthy body. This is the same energy tapped into by acupuncturists. If your body chi is blocked or stagnant, you feel or become ill. In Feng Shui, chi needs to flow unhindered in each room of your home, otherwise it may feel like an unhealthy place to be. Chi in the home can be blocked by, amongst other things, untidiness and disorganisation.

Whether you've heard of energy flow or not, having a tidy kitchen will make you feel better. If the concept of chi or energy flow is too 'out there' for you, just think of energy as a 'good vibe'.

Are you willing to spend time in your cluttered and disorganised kitchen? No. Are you willing to spend time in a clean, tidy and efficient kitchen? Yes. You probably can't wait to get in there!

See? There is a better 'vibe' in a tidy kitchen. Once the kitchen is tidy, you'll reap the benefits, mentally and physically. Your kitchen will be a super-charged space where wonderful things will happen on a daily basis.

Eat Better

Perhaps this, above all else, is what I'm getting at.

At the moment, you and your family may lament the fact that you always eat the same thing. Because nothing is organised in your pantry, fridge or cupboards, you find it too difficult to think of new dishes to prepare. It's much easier and less time consuming to cook the same dishes, especially when the kitchen is not the place you want to be. Meals are unexciting, unappealing and not as nutritious or as fresh as you'd like.

When I say 'eating better' I don't just mean nutritionally. With your tidy kitchen will come a profound sense of enjoyment of food and all that goes with it. I hope that, along with your revitalised kitchen, you will reclaim meal times with your family. Above all, good food is to be shared in good company.

You have an exciting time ahead of you. New dishes to prepare, cook and enjoy with your loved ones around you.

 Exercise

Write a list of benefits you want to see as a result of tidying and organising your kitchen.

This is a powerful exercise as it taps into your fondest wishes and desires.
You ought to be feeling positive and raring to go.

You should be feeling much more up beat after reading the above and
completing the exercises. Let's see what we can do to really get your
motivation juices flowing.

CHAPTER 4
Motivation

It's all very well talking the talk but if you lack the motivation, you will never walk the walk!

Motivation will be the driving force to get you from kitchen clutter to kitchen clear. I set out below a number of motivational exercises to energise and set you up for the task ahead.

 Exercise

Before you read any further, ask yourself how motivated you feel, right now, to declutter your kitchen. Mark yourself on a scale of one to ten; one being 'can't be bothered' and ten being 'can't wait!'. Put that mark in your notebook under the heading 'Motivation Score'. We'll revisit this score at the end of this chapter.

It's All In The Mind

Let's start where all great deeds begin: in the mind. As Henry Ford said 'whether you think you can, or whether you think you can't; you are right'.

What you think and believe affects your actions. This is because your subconscious is very obliging. It wants what you want. Unfortunately, it has no way of distinguishing what you BELIEVE from what you WANT. This is why, when you believe that you can't achieve something, you subconsciously sabotage your own efforts from the start. Your subconscious looks for ways to give you what you 'believe', which is that you 'can't'. In this way, convenient 'excuses' arise. The kids need help with their homework, you feel ill or the dog runs off with the mop. You then have the double luxury of being right about failing 'See? I told you I couldn't' and you're saved from having to try. The status quo is maintained and you can fall back into your safe, comfortable cocoon of clutter.

Even your language shows your state of mind. 'I can't do this, I am not able to do it. I don't have the time to do this. It's not my fault. I won't be able to. I'm not...I can't... I don't...I won't...not...can't...won't'. 'Oh Mon Dieu,' just listen to yourself.

I'm sure you came up with a whole lot of excuses in the exercise in Clutter

101. You are absolutely convinced that they are THE absolute exceptions that will get you out of tidying and organising your kitchen.

We need to change the way you think. Sometimes, we don't realise that we are being negative. It may take someone to point it out to us. This reminds me of a conversation I had with an acquaintance. Every few sentences, she would say she was afraid of this or frightened of that. As a consequence, she was too negative to do anything. I pointed this out to her and asked her what she was afraid of. She hadn't even realised. It transpired that she watched the news three times a day. What she saw, violence, terrorism, crime, all worried her. The answer was simple. Stop watching the news. She replied "But you have to be informed." I don't mean shutting yourself off from the world or reality, just don't let it make you negative. Once I pointed this out to her, she started to enjoy her life again.

You may be worried that you've spent so long being negative that you'll never get back to being positive. Well, here's the thing. Positive thinking is much more powerful than negative. My friend was able to turn her life around very quickly once she realised and changed her thinking pattern.

So how do you change your way of thinking? Luckily, it's very simple.

 Exercise

For the next few days, notice any negative words and/or phrases that you use habitually. If you find it difficult to identify any, ask a family member or good friend to help. Write them in your notebook. These expressions or turns of phrase can give a clue to your state of mind. Make a conscious effort to stop yourself using them. It will be difficult at first. The 'can'ts' and the 'wont's' roll out with ease. Be strong. Tell them to go away. Turn every negative comment into a positive one.

A few examples are:

'I can't tidy my kitchen' becomes 'I can and will tidy my kitchen'.
'I don't have time' becomes 'I always make time'.
'I am too tired' becomes 'I am full of energy'.

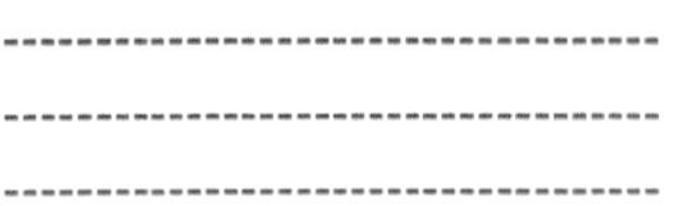

When you do this regularly, the following will happen:

Positive words will automatically replace negative words.
Positive thoughts will replace negative thoughts.
Positive actions will replace negative actions.

By focusing on what you're saying (the outward manifestation of what you're subconsciously thinking) you'll begin to turn around the way you think. This is the frame of mind you need to be in.

Affirmations

'Today is the day'. Make the decision to do something about the state of your kitchen. To give yourself encouragement, you can try affirmations. Saying strong, positive phrases can motivate you to take action. Try the following exercise now.

Read these phrases out loud and with utter conviction:

I am ready to tidy and organise!
I want to tidy!
I feel excited to take on this project!
I am decluttering now!

How do you feel after saying these affirmations? Are you more enthusiastic than lethargic? Yes? Excellent, we're getting somewhere.

♥ Tip

If you still feel unsure, say the above with more vigour and in a more assured tone. If you're worried about sounding silly, go into another room or yell the phrases into a pillow or cushion! Bet you feel better now!

✎ Exercise

Write down your most powerful affirmations (the ones you feel most comfortable saying) in your notebook inside the front cover. Say them repeatedly to yourself when you get up, when you have a spare minute during the day and when you go to bed. The more often you say them, the quicker they'll take hold.

Visualisation

Visualisation is a technique I use regularly. It is powerful and helps you accomplish your goals, whatever they may be. If you're interested, please follow me on this visualisation exercise.

 Exercise

Sit down somewhere comfortable where you won't be disturbed.
Turn your phone off.
Close your eyes.
Relax as much as you can for a few minutes.
Allow your normal level of stress to ease.
Breathe deeply.
Counting your breaths is a good way to relax.
Now, think about the goal you want to accomplish, in this case tidying and organising your kitchen.
Try to see yourself as if you were in a movie.
Watch yourself decluttering and organising the kitchen.
In this movie, you look and feel happy while doing it.
Now step into the 'you' in the movie.
You are doing the task easily, with vigour and energy.
Everything is bright and fresh.
Notice how the 'you' is feeling right now.
Feel the excitement building up inside you.
You have a huge smile on your face.
You feel contented, happy and on top of the world.
Try to see as many details as you can and see the task right through to the end.

Seeing it all done helps you to believe that it can be done.
Once you finish this exercise, open your eyes.
Let these positive feelings remain with you as long as you can.

Do this exercise a couple of times a day, or more if you want to. The more
you practice visualisation the closer to your goal you will get. Your ability to
visualise gets stronger the more you do it.

I enjoy the feeling of utter conviction I get when I visualise. The feeling
lingers long after I stop.

This kind of exercise has helped me write each of my books. I see them
already written, published and for sale. This book is no different. I can see it
finished as I write these very words. So go on, it's your turn. Visualise your
way to a tidy kitchen and then use the technique for anything else that you
want.

Vision Board

Another way to visualise is by creating a vision board.

Search online for images of kitchens that inspire you. Print them out and keep
them in full view so that they spur you on to start the project. An alternative
is to save the images on your computer and create a Word document or
slideshow. Whichever way you do it, be sure to look at it a few times a day.
You'll soon find that, if your kitchen does not match up to the ones on your
vision board, you'll want to do something about it.

Don't worry if the kitchens in the photos you choose are grander or larger
than yours. It's the thought that counts, literally. If you aspire to a grander or
larger kitchen, who's to say that you can't make that dream a reality?
Remember, a good cook can produce great food whether they are in a fully
equipped, professional kitchen or using a camping stove at base camp on
Everest! The photos are the result you're working towards.

I find vision boards a great method of realising my goals, whether that is
writing or having the home of my dreams. Why not start now and vision
board your way to a tidy kitchen?

 Exercise

Create your first vision board. Make it big and bright. The more fun you have
doing it the more the exercise will benefit you. Decorate it and put it up in a
prominent place where you can see it as often as possible. In the kitchen
would be a good place ;0)

Declutter Buddy

Many people notice that they lose momentum after a while and find it
difficult to finish a job by themselves. However, with a friend to lean on, they
perk up. They feel able to carry on because they're not alone. The friend can
act as a mentor or a crutch, somebody to rely on when the going gets tough.
Get yourself a Declutter Buddy. The best kind is someone who is also tidying
and organising their kitchen, but that isn't absolutely necessary. Agree to
support each other throughout.

Here are a few ideas to get you started:

Your buddy could be doing the same task in her own house at the same time
as you.
You can keep in contact throughout, ensuring that you both complete the
task.
Motivate each other.
Send photos to each other at each stage of the task.
Visit each other's homes. Check and admire the work done.
Make it fun or a competition.
Agree to a prize to the winner or the best 'declutterer'.
Arrange an outing to celebrate completion.

If you don't want to involve a friend, simply announcing your intention to
your household might be the spur you need. They're probably as equally to
blame for the state of the kitchen as you. So bribe or cajole them into helping
or at least taking ownership (and possession) of all their stuff you clear from
your cupboards!

 Exercise

Jot down in your notebook the names of possible Declutter Buddies and
choose the most appropriate. If you can't think of or find one, it doesn't

matter. This is just one motivational exercise of many.

Just Desserts

Another motivational technique is to promise yourself a treat for a job well done. It can be an evening of pampering at a spa, a nice meal in a favourite restaurant or a new shade of lipstick. No matter what the size of the reward, make it work for you. Look forward to it. See yourself collecting on that treat (more visualisation). This will definitely motivate you to accomplish the task. So, come on. What will your reward be?

✎ Exercise

Decide on your treat. Make it a really good one!

Write it down in big bold letters, underline it, highlight it, draw stars and smiley faces around it. The bigger, brighter and bolder you write it the more you'll be motivated to start.

When all the hard work is done, you will be glad to have a real treat to enjoy.

It's A Date

Have you ever looked back to special events you organised and wondered how you managed to get it all done? Maybe it was your wedding or a great holiday? Weren't you amazed at what you achieved? Because you were working to a firm event and date, you made yourself do all the planning and organisation required. You had no choice. It had to be done. You organised your work according to the deadline and you did it!

So what is different today with this task? Why can't you summon up the energy and enthusiasm, willpower and determination to get up and get on with it? I'll tell you why. You haven't made any firm plans yet. You haven't set any date by which this task is to be completed. It is an ever moving goal. One day, some day becomes never ever...ever!

 Exercise

Sit down now. Decide on an event, a date and guests. What can you plan to take place in your tidy and organised kitchen? It could be a get together with friends or family. How about a romantic meal with your significant other? Whatever it is, plan it in detail. The most important thing is to set a date. Make it firm. Circle it on the calendar in bold red pen. Hold yourself accountable by sending out invites or making the calls. Once committed, you have no choice but to start tidying and organising your kitchen. Now, how is that for motivation?

Write out the following in your notebook:

Event ------------------------------------
Date ------------------------------------
Guests ------------------------------------

Accountability (Light)

A sure way to get motivated is to make yourself accountable. Tell people you intend to tidy and organise your kitchen. Explain what you will do and when. Once you've done this, people will expect you to 'walk the walk'. You can't allow them to see that you haven't delivered on your promise. In this way, you're holding yourself accountable. You won't want to disappoint people but, most of all, you won't want to disappoint yourself. This is the ideal way for people who care what others think of them.

Accountability (Strong)

Social media, whether you like it or not, has a strong influence over us. Most of us are on Twitter, Facebook, Pinterest and many other networks. What an opportunity. You can use the 'Accountability' idea and up the ante by posting online what you're doing. This increases the pressure on you to deliver. Inform your entire social network about your goals and deadlines. You can state what you intend to do and post a 'before' picture (as long as it isn't too scary of course). You can state your deadline and tell people to expect an 'after' picture on that date. I'm pretty sure that your friends and followers will want to know how you get on. I'm also positive that they will support you. You may even motivate some to do the same. You can then use them as

Declutter Buddies and give each other mutual support. Result!

Accountability (Extreme)

If being accountable to family and friends is not enough motivation for you, here's a way to up the ante even further. If you have a blog, make yourself accountable on that. Publish a journal or a diary of your declutter journey from kitchen hell to kitchen heaven. You can post 'before', 'during' and 'after' photos or videos. Give detailed accounts of what you're doing. Readers can ask questions and you get feedback. This is a great way to get ideas for posts for your blog and to increase interaction on it. People love sharing and if they have ideas, these can be shared online and hopefully your blog will get more interest! Now that is a win-win. Be careful though, this is motivation on steroids. Being accountable to the world at large is scary. This is not for the faint-hearted but if you have the guts, go for it.

Please let me know which level of accountability you choose and how you get on. Let me know if you choose social media. I will Tweet my support and Like your post if I can. If you choose to blog, let me have details...I'll be watching!

 Exercise

Once you've done the exercises on motivation, repeat the exercise at the very start of this chapter. What is your Motivational Score now on a scale of one to ten? If your score was low to start with and hasn't increased dramatically, redo some of the motivation exercises. Choose the ones that appeal to you more than others. Come back when you hit eight, nine or ten.

I hope that you're now feeling sufficiently motivated to commit to the task ahead. Everyone needs to find the one motivational trigger that means the most to them, that's all. You don't need to use every single exercise, just the one that is enough to get you up and moving.

CHAPTER 5
Planning

Planning

The next three chapters are the reason why you're here. They are the very heart of this book.

It may be a cliché that if you fail to plan, you plan to fail; but it's true. You must make a decision on how to tackle your untidy kitchen and the order in which to do so.
This chapter is about formulating that plan.
The next chapter will address each individual area, appliance or equipment. After that, you will actually put the campaign into effect.
Think of this chapter as the overall campaign against your kitchen nightmare, the next chapter as the battles you'll have on the march to kitchen dream and the one after that as the actual war against the clutter.

Chunking

Have you heard of chunking? It means breaking down a large goal into smaller, achievable tasks.

This is why we're breaking the whole job of tidying and organising your kitchen into separate tasks split by area to declutter.

If you over-stretch yourself, you may find it's too difficult to achieve the goal all in one go. It's better to have little steps at which you can succeed rather than try to achieve too much and fail. That could set you back. It may be the reason you've failed before. Nothing breeds success like success. So remember, be realistic.

You may find that, when you've completed one task, it will spur you on to tackle another. Take a good look at the areas you've finished. Tell yourself that you can do this. Every now and then, stop your climb up the mountain to enjoy the view. Be happy with what you achieve. Be positive about yourself.

IMPORTANT

In your notebook, start a fresh page and head it 'Declutter Campaign'.

Now, read this chapter and the next thoroughly. Under the 'Declutter Campaign' heading, you will list all the areas mentioned that you wish to tackle to tidy and organise your kitchen and put them in order of priority for you.

Declutter Campaign Example

1/ Sink
2/ Worktops
3/ Fridge
4/ Pantry
5/ Oven
6/ Floor
7/ Dirty Drawer

I have only set out a few areas to give you an idea of how the list will work. You may have more areas or you may have less.

If you feel your fridge is fine but you really want to overhaul the oven, move it up the list. If your pantry is perfect but you need a fantastic floor, move that up the list. If you have a dirty drawer that bugs you like crazy, by all means put that at the top. Doing tasks in order of those that drive you crazy is one way to go. Alternatively, list them by time available, difficulty or level of ease. This is your campaign. There is no best or right option. As long as you tackle the problem you'll finish the job. The way you decide to proceed depends on how long you can devote to the job or what's the most urgent. You may have only one hour to spare or half a day whilst the rest of the family is out. Choose the task or tasks that best suit your needs and priorities.

Be flexible. If you have your preferred order written down, there's nothing stopping you from doing an area lower down the list, if the time or opportunity presents itself. In the above example, if you find yourself with a free half hour, you can attack your dirty drawer even if you haven't yet got the perfect pantry. You want to get to the stage where tasks are being crossed off your list. You'll get great satisfaction from seeing your list getting shorter.

The actual tidying and organising process for each area or appliance on your 'Declutter Campaign List' is as easy as 1,2,3,4: 'Empty', 'Clean', 'Declutter' and 'Organise'. Whether it's a drawer, small or large appliance, fridge, pantry or shelving, you first need to empty it, then clean, declutter and finally, organise it.

Once you have your 'Declutter Campaign List' ready, go through the same process for each task on the list. So in the example list above empty, clean, declutter and organise the sink; next empty, clean, declutter and organise the worktops and so on until you reach the end of your 'Declutter Campaign List'.

1. Empty
Step One

To be able to clean and declutter properly, you'll have to empty drawers, units or cupboards or remove the items from where they're kept. Therefore, ensuring that you have enough clear space to put things is your first task. If you haven't already done so, I suggest doing this before you clear any areas. You need enough space to set everything out so that you can see it and make decisions about whether individual items are to be kept or not. The kitchen table or worktops are perfect for this purpose.

2. Clean
Step Two

Whether you keep, give away or sell any piece, gadget or appliance, it has to be clean. Similarly, any area, unit or drawer you're decluttering needs a good clean before organising it.
Cleanliness is the prime trait of a tidy and well organised kitchen. Cleanliness is next to Food-liness!

3. Declutter
Step Three

Decluttering itself is divided into 'Decision Making', 'Sorting Out' and 'Double-Checking'.

Decision Making

First of all, something that will sound obvious but believe me is easy to overlook: you should only have in your kitchen what should be in it. Decluttering means removing all unnecessary items that have somehow found their way in. You may already have far too much of everything culinary, so you need to remove what's completely unrelated to the kitchen.

Have a box or boxes ready for 'handovers, give aways, sells or throw outs'.

Now, if an item is not being used, it will hardly be missed. To help you make a decision, if you are humming and hawing, remember the equation 'not loved + not used = not missed'. You can give away or sell pieces that you don't want to make room for those you do want. Try not to throw good things in the bin for the sake of it. Someone's 'don't want' is someone else's 'must have'.

Be strong, be fast, be thorough. 'Keeping' or 'Getting Rid Of' are the only two things that should be in your mind as you go through the decluttering process. Once you start making decisions, you'll be surprised at how much easier it becomes. Do not risk going back through the boxes marked 'handovers, give aways, sells or throw outs'. Once a decision is made, stick to it. Be a doer, not a ditherer.

♥ Tip

You could start a swap club at which everyone's invited to bring along anything they no longer need and want to exchange. As we're all into recycling these days, why not recycle gadgets, crockery and other stuff? The new owner will give the items a fresh lease of life.

♥ Tip

Instead of throwing or giving away, you could recycle everyday objects and use them in different ways.
Egg trays: put in your drawers to store pins, paperclips and elastic bands.
Old clothes pegs: use as clips to keep food packets closed in the cupboard or freezer.
Mugs: use to store cutlery on the worktop or pens next to the house phone or shopping list. How chic!
Cutlery tray: put inside your usual 'messy drawer' to keep tidy all those bits and bobs that have no other home.
Terracotta plant pots: use small ones as bread pans for individual home-made loaves or cakes.
Mismatched china cups: use to serve chocolate mousse or other creamy desserts. Your guests will love them!

Sorting Out

During the decluttering process and before you put things back into units and drawers, you'll notice crockery, food or gadgets that should be together but aren't. You may have plates in four different units, cutlery in every drawer and glasses in most of your wall cupboards. It's difficult to find things and a waste of time when they are in various places. Get them sorted. Resist the temptation to think of putting them back in the same spot. Instead, think of the most practical area for them to be altogether (for an exception to this, see the section on crockery in the next chapter). Being methodical gets the job done and makes it more enjoyable.

When sorting out, make sure that all items:

Are relevant to the kitchen.
Will be used.
If neither of the above, they are nonetheless loved.

If an item belongs in all three categories, that's the icing on the cake. You've cracked it.

If you're really not sure about any item, put it aside or into a box labelled 'Unsure' for later consideration. Once the whole kitchen has been tidied and there are still items in the 'Unsure' box, move the box into the garage or another practical place. And no, I don't mean in the kitchen. If you need something in the box, retrieve it and find a place for it. If after a time, maybe a month, you still have items left in that box, you will know you don't need them. They can then be sold, swapped or given away.

Double-checking

I can't stress the importance of double-checking your work enough. Finished emptying a unit? Check it all over. Pesky little items hide in dark and difficult to reach corners.
Finished cleaning? Grease stains, dust, have they all gone? No? Then give it another go with the sponge until these stains are history.
Finished sorting out? Make sure that you've put all the items you no longer need into the appropriate box (or the bin).

Try to avoid thinking 'oh never mind, that will do'. Set the standard high and stick to it. This way, your kitchen will soon gleam and sparkle like those on your vision board. If the cupboard is clean, start putting items back in an orderly fashion. Think about organising them in baskets, trays or containers to help you clean faster in the future.

4. Organise
Step Four

This last stage consists of organising decluttered and cleaned units, drawers and shelving with objects which have been cleaned and decluttered themselves. Take a moment to decide where these items should reside. The criteria should be practical and easy locations. These all important organisational decisions will dictate whether or not your kitchen is practical and user-friendly. Organising your units and shelves is not a mindless task. Think about it now so that it doesn't worry you later. Much of the work will have been done at the 'Sorting Out' stage so 'Organisation' should be a breeze. There is still time to change your mind when you actually see things in situ.

CHAPTER 6
How To Tidy And Clean By Area

This chapter is primarily about compiling your 'Declutter Campaign List'. It will also show you how to attack each area and appliance in your 'Declutter Campaign'. Each area is presented alphabetically so that you can locate each one easily. Remember to write out your 'Declutter Campaign List' in your notebook in order of priority for your situation, always bearing in mind some flexibility may be required.

I set out below the four-step plan (Empty, Clean, Declutter, Organise) for each different area and/or appliance and give more information pertinent to each.

Ceiling

The ceiling is an area that very often gets neglected. As it's above our heads, we don't see it and, well, maybe we want to ignore it. However, like everything else, it requires a good clean now and again, even if it's only once a year. It's amazing how much dust finds its way up to the ceiling and how many pesky spiders make webs in corners.

Empty
If you have pendant lights and ceiling fans, they should be dismantled, if possible, to clean around them. If working at height, make sure you have a good sturdy step ladder and someone else is around to hold it for you.

Clean
My first task is always to get a broom and sweep out the cobwebs in the corners. I even give the whole ceiling a sweep over to remove any dust. Light fixtures and ceiling fans are easier to clean if taken down and dismantled than cleaned whilst in situ. They harbour plenty of dust and more cobwebs. Light fixtures tend to fill up with dead bugs so give them a good hoover out and thorough washing. Fans can spray dust all over the kitchen if left dirty for too long. Give particular attention to the blades. Dust and grease could be an inch thick up there. Wash or wipe the cord of the fan, if it has one. Dry everything well.

Always be careful when washing electrical switches and sockets. Use damp, not wet, cloths and make sure switches and sockets are set to 'off' before cleaning them. To make absolutely sure, turn the switch off at the mains, when washing down.

Give the ceiling itself a good wipe. If it needs it, give it a coat of matt paint too. There are various kitchen paints available which resist moisture and mould. This will have the effect of making the kitchen look much brighter and fresher.

Declutter
Check that all light bulbs work. It isn't pleasant cooking in the gloom. There isn't much to declutter here, thank goodness so, unless you are giving the ceiling a lick of fresh paint, this won't take much time. This task can be easily slotted into any time that comes available.

Organise
Replace bulbs that are blown. Put back all the parts of the light fittings and ceiling fans. The kitchen should look and feel much brighter now.

♥ Tip
When washing above head height, water runs down your arm and saturates your clothes. It's not a nice feeling to work whilst damp so wrap a tea towel comfortably around your wrist or tightly around the mop handle. That will absorb any excess water and keep you dry.

Consider List

Remember your 'Consider List'? Now is the time to think about all the items on it and whether you want to keep them.

Empty them all out from where they are kept. Give them a good dusting and wash if necessary. Remove all items you are sure you no longer want. This will immediately clear space in your kitchen. Think about whether you want to sell them or give them away to family friends or charity.

This will be a very good job done. Give yourself an extra pat on the back right now.

Crockery And China

This is not an 'area' of the kitchen but a category of items that regularly need tidying and organising. Decluttering categories of things should be approached in exactly the same way as an area.

Empty

Okay, you've decided to tackle your crockery and china. You should have a clear space somewhere, on the kitchen table or worktops. Fish out all your cups, saucers, mugs, plates, platters, side dishes, bowls, serving dishes, the lot! Every single piece of crockery and china should be out of the cupboards, drawers, units, dressers and anywhere else they may be stashed. Once they're laid out, you get an idea of what you've got.

Clean

Clean the pieces that have not been used for a while. Fill up your sink with soapy water and get to it. Unless very dirty, a quick wipe and dry is all they'll need. While washing and drying, check each piece for breakages and cracks. Start addressing your mind as to whether you want to keep it and its set or not. Alternatively, stack them in the dishwasher (after checking for breakages) and wash on a quick cycle.

Declutter

Now that your crockery and china are clean and dry, sort them all out by set and/or type. If you have stacks of plates but only ever use the top ones, this could be a sign that you have too many. Keeping a dinner service all together makes sense. If it has many pieces damaged or missing, you may choose to give it away. Alternatively, if mismatched china is your thing, keep it.

I suggested earlier keeping only what you regularly use and pieces that you cherish. I have to admit that, as a French chic fan, I use vintage mismatched plates daily. I'm a great believer in things earning their keep. The only exception is a couple of my great grandmother's old plates which I display on the dresser. I keep them because they remind me of her. But, anything else not earning its keep is given away if it's still usable, binned if it's not. Now is the time for you to make the decision whether each piece is earning its keep or just taking up valuable space.

Organise

While restocking the units with your crockery and china, consider putting them in the most appropriate place. You don't have to keep all your china and crockery in one spot. A dinner set can be split for reasons of practicality. For example, as I prefer to serve food at the table, I keep the plates and bowls in my French dresser, close to the dining table. The serving dishes are stored in the kitchen units, close to the hob and oven. If you prefer to serve directly on to plates and carry them to the table, keep these in the kitchen. Another reason to keep plates and serving dishes separate is that, while I'm cooking, my husband can lay the table and stay out of my hair.

♥ Tip

Tea and coffee mugs can be housed close to the kettle and cafetière for instant brews.

♥ Tip

Allowing yourself to use the best every day could be the beginning of a new you; one who feels she's worth more than she used to think. So, start in the kitchen. Use good china. Eat delicious food. Let this new spirit spill out into the rest of the house and your life. Dig out your sweetest smelling candles from the back of the drawer and light them for your next bath. Wear your new shoes next time you go out. Wear your best clothes. This will revitalise you, give you more confidence and make you feel special.

♥ Tip

To remove brown tea or coffee stains from your cups, first wet the stain with white vinegar. Next, scrub it out with a paste of baking soda on a sponge until any brown mark is gone. Rinse well.

Cutlery And Utensils

This is another category of kitchenware rather than an area. Again, treat exactly as you would an area of the kitchen.

Empty
Cutlery and utensils are fiddly and knives may be sharp so be careful when handling them. Remove them all from their drawers and storage pots. Lay them out on a flat surface.

Clean
Now is the chance to give them a good wash and polish. Remove any stubborn, dried up food that may be stuck on. If you have any silver or silver plate, use appropriate cleaning products. Dry them with a clean cloth. Make them sparkle. I have an antique carving set from my paternal great-

grandmother which I polish regularly. I find polishing therapeutic.

Now, on to the cutlery drawer itself. Every few weeks, I empty and clean mine. It's surprising how much dust, crumbs and fluff collect in there. I pull the cutlery tray out completely, shake it directly into the bin and then give it a good wash. I hoover out the inside of the drawer with the long thin hoover attachment. I finish off by giving a quick wipe with a dry cloth. I then replace the tray. If you use storage pots for your utensils, give them a good wash too, inside and out.

Declutter
Look at each piece carefully. Make sure that handles aren't broken or loose, knives are sharp, tines on forks are straight and spoons haven't been got at by Uri Geller. (If you're too young to remember him, look him up on the internet!) Now's the time to get rid of those that don't pass muster.

Organise
Store all cutlery and utensils close to the place you need them. Put cutlery out of the way inside a drawer. Place utensils away or in full view, either in a pretty storage pot or hung from hooks. I keep my most used utensils in a steel pot next to the hob. They provide a practical display, ready at a moment's notice. The cutlery and the rest of my utensils are kept in a tray in a large drawer.

Dishwasher

The first of what I would call the major appliances. The dishwasher is a true labour saving device but one that needs to be kept in good order to get the most out of it.

Empty
If you do have one of these handy labour and argument saving machines, well done you. Empty it completely. This doesn't just mean last night's dishes! I would also recommend taking out all the trays, baskets and moving parts in the well of the machine. Refer to the manual for full instructions on how to dismantle the cleaning heads and rotating blades.

Clean
From time to time, your dishwasher will need cleaning. Despite it being used

to clean dishes, you'll find that it gets grubby inside as well as out. You may notice a build up of grease and fat, food and water stains and even mould. As I believe that prevention is better than cure, regularly run the machine through a full cycle with a good dose of white vinegar inside. This will keep your machine clean and running well.

Once every couple of months, dismantle the baskets and the rotating blades. Check these for blockages as bits of food may get lodged in there. You can take the blades apart almost entirely to clear out trapped food. Occasionally, you may need to use a piece of wire to get at particles of food trapped in spray nozzles or at the very end of the blades, pipes or tubes. Empty and clean the filter. Put them all back together.

For a thorough clean, run an empty machine through a full cycle with a cup of bleach in the dispenser. Don't worry, it won't harm it. You can also buy cleaning tablets to put into the machine and run it through a cycle to clean the inside thoroughly. It's up to you. However, read first what the manual recommends.

To finish off, wipe the sides and front of the door, and you're done.

Declutter and Organise
If any parts need replacing, go get them or order them online. Nothing is worse than a machine that can't be used or doesn't work properly for lack of maintenance. Put everything back in and check the moving parts work properly. 'Voilà', ready to go.

Drawers

Drawers are ideal declutter time-fillers. If you haven't got much time, you can always work on one drawer to keep the kitchen campaign going.

Empty
Why is there always a messy drawer in everyone's home? Lurking within are objects we don't know what to do with. So, into this drawer they go. There could be anything, such as boxes of matches, birthday candles, phone chargers, open seed packets, pencils, leaky pens, paperclips, old keys, elastic bands and take away menus. You'll also find all manner of other bits and bobs that serve no immediate nor useful purpose.

If you can't open any drawer without giving it a good yank, it's high time for a declutter. So, empty the contents of the drawer onto a clear surface. You may be surprised at what you find.

Clean

Once the drawer is empty, give it a good clean. Hoover into corners and use a damp or dry cloth to wipe it out, not forgetting the sides and underneath. Have a look at the runners to make sure they're not caked in fluff. If they don't run smoothly, a squirt of WD40 works wonders on modern runners. On wooden drawers, rub a cold, unlit candle over the runners. The wax acts as a lubricant and the drawer should run smoothly.

Declutter

When it comes to tidying your messy drawer, have a box for members of the household to hand. Fill it with their things. Present the box to them afterwards, gift wrapped if you wish.

If you can do without the contents of the drawer then it's time to consign them to the bin, charity shop or give them away. We keep these things in the faint hope that, one day, we may well need the out of date take away menu, old phone chargers, rusty keys or used birthday candles. It's high time to acquire a discerning eye for what we really need. These things generally cost only a few pennies to replace anyway, so why do we keep them? We do it out of habit. Reclaim the space and a whole drawer in which you can put things you really need. Do you have a messy drawer? Not for long, I hope.

Organise

Now, you can put what you're keeping back in tidily. Try to find a box or cutlery tray that fits the size of the drawer. It makes keeping that drawer tidy and clean much easier. If you haven't got a tray, consider using eggs boxes or margarine tubs. These may not look chic but they're better than having loose items moving around in the drawer. If you've thrown everything out, consider giving this drawer another use.

Extractor Fan

A much neglected appliance in my view and one that comes in for regular punishment.

Empty

There's nothing to empty here, but you may wish to remove the filters for cleaning and bulbs if they need replacing. If the extractor fan has become an extra shelf, replete with knick-knacks, now's the time to clear them off.

Clean
After the oven, extractor fans are the next most difficult things to clean. They have bits that come off, slide around, press in and out and twirl around. They also take the brunt of what comes off the top of your stove, hob or gas rings (or hot plates if we're talking about Aga owners). If you do a lot of frying, it's likely that they'll be caked in oil. The filters of course can be cleaned or replaced. If they are dishwasher-safe, all the better. If not, it's back to good old elbow grease. Use a de-greaser to attack the whole hood, on the outside as well as underneath. Use a toothbrush to get into nooks, crannies and any other parts that a cloth just won't get to. The top may require some attention if it's above eye level and regularly gets 'forgotten' (cough cough!). If you do this often, maybe every couple of weeks, you'll keep the grease in check. I pass a damp cloth over mine after a heavy cooking session. It takes only moments, but prevents fatty build-up and lessens a fire risk.

Just a word here about the outside vent. As it's outside, it may get overlooked; but if it's in an outside area that's used regularly, don't forget to give that a good clean as well. The grease and grime has to go somewhere and a greasy, grimy vent in your garden doesn't look very appealing.

Declutter and Organise
Extractor fans were not designed to be used as shelving, so leave the top clear. Just put the filters back in, once they're clean and dry. Turn the fan on to check if it's in good working order and it's ready for the next cooking session.

Floor

We walk over it every day and hardly give it a thought. However, the expression that a 'floor is so clean that you could eat your dinner off it' is a reminder that it too needs regular TLC.

Empty
Unless you're Shaker, you are bound to have stools, bins, vegetable racks,

school bags, dog bowls and other things that take up floor space. Everything has to be cleared out of the way for you to have uninterrupted access to the entire floor area. There is nothing more irritating than trying to clean a floor when you have to keep moving things around.

Clean
The type of products you use depend on the type of floor you have. Whether for linoleum, tiles, slates or wood, use the proper cleaning products.
I hoover first to pick up all the dust, crumbs and fluff. Use the available hoover nozzles to get into all corners and spaces. If there are gaps between fridge, oven and units, find some way to get in there to suck up all the dropped crumbs.
There's no better alternative than the good old bucket and mop to bring a kitchen floor back to its sparkly best. Some types of flooring will need polishing or sealing after being washed. I give my natural slates a coat of special oil to give them a really deep lustre.

Declutter
Floor space in a kitchen is at a premium. When carrying knives or pots and pans of boiling water, you don't want any trip hazards in the way. Your triangle of work (see Chapter 8) should be kept clear.

Organise
After sorting out what should or shouldn't be in the kitchen, it's time to put things back. A bare kitchen floor is best. Having said that, some things have to be there, such as a free-standing bin, a stool or vegetable rack. Little Johnny's gym bag can be handed to him and the hamster cage can be moved to somewhere more suitable. Consider whether cat litter trays really belong in the kitchen.

Freezer

The freezer can be a place where you cram in as much as you can and shut the door quickly. As already mentioned, offers in the shops make us buy more than we need. Buying discounted foods that can be frozen makes sense as they will keep for much longer. But even frozen foods may not look or taste quite as good if kept too long. If your freezer isn't efficient, there is a chance that, over time, there may be some thaw and refreeze of some foodstuffs. Further, you only have to leave the door slightly ajar for a few minutes (or cram too much in so that it doesn't close properly) for the temperature to rise enough in hot weather to spoil some of the contents.

With too much in the freezer, you may never get to see what's at the back or bottom. You may only ever grab what's on top. Foods that have been in there too long are wasted and may be just plain inedible when you come to defrost them. Regularly go through what you have. Every few months, try to finish what's in there. Alternatively, simply turn the contents over so what was at the back or at the bottom comes to the front or top. At least, it then has a chance of getting eaten.

Empty
You need to plan the freezer decluttering in advance. Aim to run the contents of the freezer down as much as possible. On the day, prepare an ice box or boxes and transfer the freezer contents into them to reduce the risk of defrosting. Any food that starts defrosting will have to be consumed and not refrozen. This is a task that needs to be completed quickly. So get all you need at the ready before starting.

Clean
Once empty, the freezer can be cleaned. It's amazing how easily plastic bags can split. You may find frozen peas and sweet corn all over the place. Brush out all debris and loose ice. Give the baskets and compartments a good clean too. If they can be taken out and washed, all the better. Try not to leave the door open for longer than necessary. Read the manual about defrosting at recommended intervals, although new appliances don't need it.

Declutter
As you swiftly transfer foods from freezer to ice box, decide there and then whether any can be used that day or the next. If so, put them in the fridge to defrost. If there are any that look off, or well beyond their freezer life, don't hesitate to throw them out. Have a couple of good, thick garden refuse bags ready to take these. You don't want defrosting and rotting meat or fish in your bin for too long. Double-bagging will help to keep smells in and vermin out.

Organise
Whether your freezer is part of your fridge or a large separate chest, grouping foods together makes for ease of retrieval. Meats, vegetables, fruit, sauces

and herbs have their own place. If you do your own preserves or freeze your leftovers, I recommend that you name and date them on a label or directly on the bag. The oldest food should be at the top or front of your freezer to be used the soonest.

♥ Tip

Only buy for your freezer what can be eaten in the next few weeks. That way you won't buy too much and the risk of things laying forgotten is reduced.

♥ Tip

Avoid opening and closing the freezer unnecessarily or, worse, leaving the door open for a few minutes. Doing this will increase the temperature of the interior and reduce the life-span of your frozen goods.

♥ Tip

Most foods can be frozen. This includes raw and cooked meats, fish, shellfish, vegetables, fruit and even cheeses. Although some fruits will lose their consistency or colour, such as berries, bananas or apples, they can still be used for smoothies and pies. Try it out if unsure.

Fridge

I love my fridge. Looking after it and its contents is one of the most important jobs in the kitchen. If you're happy at any time for a stranger to open your fridge, you know you're a tidy kitchen queen.

Empty
Like the freezer, decluttering the fridge requires planning. All the food needs to be kept cool, while you clean the interior. Empty the contents of the fridge into ice boxes. Once all the food, drinks and condiments are out, you need to remove the drawers, shelves, sliders and divisions. Stack these at the sink, ready for washing. Now, cleaning can take place in earnest.

Clean
Cleaning the fridge is not seen as the most enjoyable task. However, it has to be done. Many people ask how often they should clean their fridge. The answer is that you should clean it whenever you need to. It isn't a case of how often but when. I say you can't clean your fridge too often. Just before

you do your big shop, which is probably weekly, is a good idea. You may not need to clean your fridge every day, although if ingredients get knocked over or spilled, you should wipe it straight away.

Use cleaning products you're comfortable with. For a natural product, a mixture of equal parts water and white vinegar in a spray bottle is fine and can be kept handy. To remove tough stains, use a paste made of baking soda and water. Alternatively, there are many other products on the market.

Start cleaning the fridge from the top down. That means the very top. You know, the place that acts as an extra shelf for stacks of pans, plates, mixing bowls and gadgets in boxes and even pot plants. If you have an integrated fridge, this will not apply to you but, if it's free standing, the outside definitely needs to be given a good clean. If you use a lot of oil in your cooking, the top may well be covered in a thin film of grease, if it hasn't been cleaned for a while. Of course, the stuff that was stored on top needs to be washed as well.

For stainless steel fridges, you can buff the outside with a proprietary spray. Finish with a cloth dipped in a little baby oil to bring back that showroom shine. Buff well to remove as much oil as you can.

Okay, outside done, now for the inside. After a good wash of the roof, walls and floor, rinse and towel dry. Give a good scrub to all the grids and other internal supports that hold the compartments and shelves. Dirt and mould can gather in there and ruin a good clean. A nail brush or toothbrush can get into all the little nooks and crannies that a cloth can't. Now, there's one area that you may have forgotten. That is the seal around the door! It tends to get mucky and grimy. It can be a devil to clean as it tends to be made out of corrugated rubber or plastic. Get your trusty toothbrush (the one for cleaning your house, not your teeth) and have a go at the seal.

Now, over to the sink to wash the drawers, shelves and compartments. Give them a really good wash and rinse. Dry them and put them back in. If you feel that you need more height in some areas, try moving the shelves and other compartments around.

Every once in a while, you'll have to move a free-standing fridge out from its station to clean behind it and along the sides. Getting the fridge out is necessary as the worktop may run up to but not completely seal around the side of the fridge. Food can easily fall down the gaps and attract vermin. So, enlist the help of a strong friend, pull it out and give the area behind the fridge a good scrub and wash down.

Declutter and Organise
People tend to overestimate the amount of food they eat in a week. They buy in large amounts 'just to be on the safe side' or so that they don't have to go back to the shops. However, they end up throwing unused food away, every week. The shopping trip is a weekly chore for most. This can be for many reasons. Most of us shop only at the weekend. Why not try to do the weekly shop during one evening instead of the weekend? There'll be less crowds and you'll get it out of the way for the weekend.

Decluttering your fridge starts at the supermarket. Try not to buy too many of the same perishable items or too large packets of ingredients. The BOGOF (buy one get one free) offers seem tempting in the shops with their large, red stickers, but can you really use five tubs of margarine before they go off? This will undoubtedly lead to wastage.

Taking the contents of the fridge out is a good chance to see what you need to buy in your next weekly shop. So this task serves a dual purpose, cleaning the fridge and writing your shopping list.

Before placing the contents back into the fridge, throw away foodstuffs past their 'use by' date. This is especially important for meat and fish. They can make you seriously ill if allowed to expire. Don't take the chance. Place the food that you need to eat quickly at the front where it's easily spotted. Clean around the lid of any jars or bottles which have dribbles down the side (neither appealing nor hygienic). You should really do this after each use. If you have little jars or packets, collect them into a Tupperware container with a lid and keep them in that. That way, they'll all be kept in one tidy place.

♥ Tip
When organising any area of your home, keep in mind that everything should make your life easier and simpler, not more complicated. Keeping it simple is practical.

♥ Tip

To avoid degreasing the top of your fridge in future, cover it with sheets of newspaper. This way, the grease will be prevented from settling on the surface. Just replace the newspaper once a month.

♥ Tip

If you're unsure of what goes where in the fridge, refer to the manual instruction booklet that came with it. Manuals contain a wealth of information about your fridge that I bet you never even knew!

♥ Tip

If you think you've bought too much food in bulk, don't leave them in the fridge to go bad. Separate and stack them in the freezer to avoid wastage.

♥ Tip

Keep half a lemon or a cup of baking soda on a shelf in the fridge to keep odours at bay.

♥ Tip

Even in a fridge, mould can develop. Be on the lookout for this health hazard. If you see small black spots, it's time for a good clean. Hopefully, your fridge never gets to that stage. But it can happen to anyone if they've been away for a while.

♥ Tip

If you're going away on holiday, try to finish off as much food from your fridge as you can, to avoid wastage when you get back. Declutter and clean it before you go.

Gadgets

When it comes to gadgets, our 'empty, clean, declutter, organise' method may not apply. You still have to get them all out as they may need sprucing up, but the main consideration is whether you're going to keep them or not.

Only keep things that help you prepare, cook, serve a meal, make your life easier or that you love. For instance, what's the point of a gadget that saves you seconds preparing a dish but takes you 30 minutes to dismantle and clean?

Does that make sense to you?

Do you have such gadgets?

Do you find that they take more of your time than they save?

Have you stopped using them for that very reason?

If so, get rid of them, especially if they take up a whole drawer or half a unit. You may feel a sense of relief when they're gone!

If your kitchen is on the small side or seriously lacking in storage space, going through any gadgets you've accumulated is essential.

To prepare and cook delicious food, you don't need a vast array of gadgets, electrical appliances or tools that are never used. Will your cooking be any less successful if you have a smaller number of gadgets? I say with all my heart, 'Non'!

You may be attached to some items, even if they serve no purpose. For me, the item that I can't let go of is my mother's sugar tongs. We no longer use sugar cubes in my house but these tongs are a little something of hers that remains in my kitchen. They're not silver or particularly rare or expensive. They're a little keepsake that make me smile and remind me of my childhood. In addition to this, they don't take much space in the drawer.

As mentioned elsewhere, for every item in your kitchen, except those very few sentimental pieces, you should be able to answer these simple questions:

Does this item help me cook?

How often do I use it?

If the answer to the first question is, 'it doesn't', then you may want to rethink why you still have it.

If the answer to the second question is 'hardly ever' or 'I can't remember when I last used it', ask yourself why you're holding onto it.

If it's for looking, not cooking, it's for ditching. Unless of course, as for my mother's sugar tongs, they're for loving.

Saving Time

The electrical appliances you need daily are your cooker/hob, oven, fridge/freezer, microwave, food processor, blender, whisk, scales and kettle. And even then, I could declutter even further by omitting the microwave, food processor, electric whisk and kettle. If you're steering towards minimalism, you could do without these, although there will be more to do by hand. Time is an issue for all of us and the appliance or gadget you ditch in favour of doing it all by hand may cost you in terms of time. So, only get rid of what you don't use, or you may become stressed due to lack of time. You may want to keep your bread-maker for instance if you bake regularly, at the very least weekly, and prefer not to do it by hand, to save time.

Regular Use

Keep gadgets only when you are sure that you'll use them regularly. If not, they will forever take up space in your cupboards, on your shelves or worktops. For instance, I have a food processor and a heavy stand mixer. The food processor takes up a lot of space with its myriad accessories but I managed to make room for it all inside a cupboard so that it doesn't clutter my worktop. One of its many uses is in winter, every two days, to make soup. It chops all the vegetables in less than a minute and blends the soup once cooked. However, I tend to use the same accessories over and over again and some I don't even know what they're for. So, I'm thinking of decluttering these too. Be careful when ditching part of a set. You can guarantee that, as soon as it's gone, you suddenly find a use for it. Once gone, it can be difficult to replace without buying the whole set again!

My much loved, super heavy stand mixer, remains on my worktop. It's a thing of beauty: all stainless steel and enamel. I use it all the time as baking is a passion of mine. 'Fondant au chocolat' anyone?

It can be quite difficult to resist buying kitchen gadgets, I know. Kitchen gadgets and appliances are to cooks what handbags and shoes are to fashionistas. I admit I've succumbed on occasions, for shoes and handbags too! But now, everything in my kitchen serves a purpose, even my husband, and if he doesn't, he is ushered out 'tout de suite'!

In the spirit of decluttering, I'm going to ask you a question. Hands up who regularly uses a chocolate fountain, a cupcake machine or popcorn maker? They sounded like a great idea at the time you bought them, 'n'est ce pas'?

You may even have used them once or twice. However, once you noticed how much time was needed to dismantle all the parts to clean, you soon stopped using them. You probably forgot about these gadgets for ages until, one day, you found them when looking for something else. How many of us have rediscovered some gadget when doing some decluttering and remarked: "Oh! I forgot I had this!" or "I don't remember ever using this" or "Why on earth did I buy this?" Or even "What is THIS?" Does this sound familiar? You may now be wondering why you kept it for so long. Out of sight, out of mind, by any chance?

If you have any of the following electrical tools, but your kitchen is lacking space, let's look at the alternatives:

Gadget:
Chocolate fountain
Alternative:
I know, I know, you can't beat the theatrics of a chocolate fountain. All that warm, creamy chocolate sauce flowing deliciously over the fountain, into which you dip your gooey marshmallows or juicy strawberries… divine! Well, this may prove as difficult for you as it is for me but let's try to stop the dreaming (for a moment at least). Instead, simply melt the chocolate and cream in a saucepan. Serve the chocolate sauce in pretty cups or ramekins. Keep them warm in a 'bain marie' (hot water bath). Problem solved! It'll taste the same, albeit without the theatrics, wastage, fuss and washing up for the host, in other words, you. I'm sure that after you've experienced the amount of washing and fiddling that goes into cleaning this gadget, you'll surely prefer the saucepan alternative.

Gadget:
Electric knife
Alternative
Your electric knife requires less effort to carve with than ordinary knives. However, these uncovered, fast moving blades scare me. I'd worry that I or a child might end up with a finger missing. Brrr, it gives me the chills. The alternative is simple. How much more of an effort does it really require to carve a roast chicken with a carving knife or slice a baguette with a bread knife? Purchase good quality carving knives. Look after them and sharpen them regularly. This will keep them sharp enough for any job. Keep them in a

block on your worktop or on a magnetic strip on the wall above the hob. There, they are close at hand but out of the reach of little fingers.

Gadget:
Ice-cream maker
Alternative:
The bowl of the ice cream maker has to be placed inside a freezer for a few hours before making ice cream. There are two downsides to this: the first one is that you can't make ice cream on the spur of the moment. The second is that the bowl takes too much room in your freezer. But there is an alternative. Of course, you can buy tubs of ready made ice cream but many of us love mixing our own flavours and ingredients. It always taste ten times better. You can make quick ice cream with just a simple custard mixture or by whisking cream. Add your preferred flavour, such as fruit, nuts or chocolate and put this into the freezer. You can whisk this mixture after one or two hours to avoid ice crystals forming, but you don't have to. Easy peasy ice cream or 'crème glacée': great for kids and adults alike when it's really hot. You could even buy lolly sticks, pour the mixture inside freezer-proof glasses or cups, and stand the sticks in the mixture. 'Et voilà!' Ready-made lollipops for the children to run around the garden with.

My husband's alternative is to buy a tub of vanilla ice cream. Let it melt until mushy. Add in fruit, nuts, honey, or chocolate sauce, chocolate bar chunks, marshmallows and any other ingredients you like. Put it back in the tub and refreeze. Of course, a certain amount of the ice cream has to be eaten there and then! 'Quelle surprise'!

Gadget:
Cupcake machine
Alternative:
The alternative, you've guessed it, is to use cupcake moulds. Pour the batter into the paper cases and that's it, done. If you have a large family, save on electricity by baking large batches. Keep them in airtight containers for a few days or freeze them. Cake moulds don't take much space in your kitchen cupboards or drawers. You'll save on washing up too, as gadgets always have all sorts of nooks and crannies for bits of food to cling to. By using paper cases, you may not even need to wash the mould.

Gadget:
Coffeemaker/Espresso machine
Alternative:
I hope I won't alienate coffee machine lovers here. If you get easily upset, please look away now.

I think that some people are more in love with these beautiful espresso and cappuccino machines than the actual coffee they produce. I do agree however that these Italian babies are works of art: shiny chrome, sleek design and gorgeous colours to match your kitchen decor. I admire them too. Very retro chic, well done you clever marketing people. The thing is, not only are they bulky but most of them require coffee capsules that add up to a fair amount of money, by the end of the year. I priced one famous brand online for this book and at that time it showed £3.30 ($5.36) for 10 capsules + P & P of £3.00 ($4.87). Goodness! That works out at 63 pence ($1.02) per cup! When you work out the hefty price tag of the machines alone, which can go into the hundreds of pounds and then add in the price of the capsules, you can see how your caffeine habit becomes a very expensive one. It's not just the caffeine that'll wake you up in the morning, it's the price of your cappuccino!

What I'm asking is:
What do you do when you run out of capsules, as they only contain ten in a pack? Do you then make a cup of tea instead?
What will it cost to repair your machine and put in new parts, doubtless imported from Italy? How long will it take?

If the cost alone doesn't deter you, please go ahead and enjoy your coffee machine.
For those of you who'd rather simplify their life, help their bank balance, gain worktop space and time, a simple cafetière is the answer. This isn't an electric gadget, it's a French press coffee maker. It consists of a glass jug in a metal sleeve or holder, a handle and a metallic plunger with a reusable filter. Every component is easily pulled apart for washing and is dishwasher safe. Cafetières are extremely easy to use and don't require an instruction manual. Ground coffee is placed at the bottom of the jug, hot water poured over it, stir if you wish, cover with the plunger/filter and wait a few minutes to brew. Enjoy the aroma as it fills your kitchen or wafts over the breakfast table. Then comes the wonderful moment of pushing the plunger down slowly. My

siblings and I always used to fight over the honour of making the press! Your coffee is then ready to be poured into your cup, filtered as it goes. There is no need to buy filters and it's cheap to replace if the glass jar breaks. A winner! For an authentic French flavour and experience, sprinkle a tablespoon of 'chicorée' granules into the glass jar on top of the ground coffee. This brings out the flavour of the coffee and is guaranteed to 'perc' up your day.

Here are a few other gadgets that may gather dust after only a couple of uses:

Candy floss maker
Popcorn maker
Novelty-shaped ice cube tray

I'm sure that you may be able to add to this list after a quick glance through your cupboards.

By all means, keep these gadgets if you wish but seriously consider the space to use ratio, first.

Hob

Empty, Clean, Declutter and Organise
There may be nothing to empty or clear from the hob unless you store pans on it, so we'll concentrate on cleaning.

If you own a gas cooker, the fiddly bits that support the pans over the gas rings will be a pain. Most, however, come apart easily and cover only one or two rings. You may get away with only cleaning the part on which you cook unless of course the pan really boiled over or exploded!

Electric ceramic hobs are the easiest to keep clean. A quick wipe is all they need. If anything has dried and caked on the surface, there are many proprietary products that will do the job painlessly.

Aga owners will already know to use a wire brush to scrub off their hot plates and remove the dust with a soft brush. The plate covers and top can be wiped down with a damp sponge or cloth.

Clean, or at least wipe, your hob after any spills and after every use. Keeping your hob clean daily is better than an hour spent at the end of the week scraping off seven days worth of caked-on food. A little and often is always better and really takes no time at all. Once the habit is acquired, you won't mind spending the minute it takes. It also adds to the overall clean look of your kitchen. Cleaning the hob is a quick job that you can squeeze in between other tasks.

Microwave Oven

Most of us own a microwave oven and use it every day. These appliances get dirty very quickly as liquids easily boil over, splashing the turntable and inside walls. Once these spills dry, they are hard to dislodge, with much crooking of your head, bending over and moving your hand in unnatural movements. Really, they're practical to use but very impractical to clean.

Empty
There's nothing to clear out from the microwave (I hope) except the turntable.

Clean
Give a good wipe to the door, top, sides and underneath of the oven. Don't forget the feet as they could be caked in dust and grime. Now, clean the inside thoroughly. Do not use any scourer, only a gentle sponge or cloth. Wipe it dry. Leave the door open to air. Wash the turntable or stack it in the dishwasher.

Declutter and Organise
Replace the clean, dry turntable inside.

Your microwave is now fit for work.

 Tip
Before cleaning dried up spills, microwave a cup of water and lemon juice on high until boiling. Leave it inside the oven for a few minutes. The steam generated will loosen up the stains. Then wipe off the spills. You'll be left with a nice lemony smell and a clean microwave.

Oven

'Aaaaaargh!' I hear you say. There can't be many more unpleasant jobs than cleaning the oven. For that reason, it's one of those tasks that gets done the least often. Raise your hand those of you who enjoy it! If you do, please tell us how you make it fun. I know of one good friend who avoids cooking in the oven at all to save having to clean it! Now this is extreme, but you can see the logic. Luckily, there are many products on the market that make this hated job much easier than it used to be in our mothers' day.

Some of you may clean their oven once a week, once a month or once in a blue moon. The amount of effort increases dramatically the longer you leave it, so doing the task more often will actually save you time in the long run. Leave it too long and you may have to hire a sand blaster!

Empty
First of all, remove the collection of baking trays and pans that always gather inside. Slide out the grills and supports. Put all these to soak in the sink, with hot water. Adding washing powder (not washing up liquid) helps lift off the burnt-on spills and grime.

Clean
The amount of grease and grime depends on how much you use the oven and what you cook. If you don't clean it regularly, the oven will burn all that was spilled in it last time. Instead of the aroma of succulent roast chicken, you'll get the stench of burnt pork or beef. This not only ruins that yummy cooking smell but may also taint the chicken.

Right now, the smug Aga or Rayburn owners amongst you can sit back and crow that cleaning the oven is a task they don't have to carry out. One of the many benefits of these beautiful things is that, as the ovens are always on, the spilled food and splashes inside are carbonised completely. All the owners need to do is sweep their ovens out with a wire brush occasionally, 'et voilà'. I do envy you.

Anyway, back to those of us with conventional ovens. There are some great products on the market these days. My favourite is one that you simply apply with the brush provided over the surfaces of the oven; leave this gel on for the recommended time and then just wipe off. I'm afraid the only alternative is backache and elbow grease.

Oh and as a 'reward', once the oven is sparkling, you can scrub off the grills and pans until they shine.

Declutter And Organise
Take a look at all the pans and trays for your oven. Get rid of any that never get used or are damaged or buckled. Treat yourself to new ones if required.

Pantry

Some of you may be lucky enough to have a pantry, that's a separate room for all your tinned and packet foodstuffs. Whether it's a cupboard (either one or many) or something that would grace Downton Abbey, a good pantry is just as magical a place as the fridge.

My mother's pantry was a wonderful place when I was growing up. There were summer fruits preserved in jams, autumn nuts and berries sealed in jars ready for winter roasts and tins of then luxury things such as exotic fruits that are common today. The pantry and fridge are the magician's hat out of which marvellous things can be pulled to create wonderful culinary wizardry.

When it comes to decluttering the pantry, this is a big task. Give yourself plenty of time.

Empty
Have some bin bags ready for any items that are seriously degraded and should be thrown out immediately. Clear out your pantry (or cupboards) of all foods. If there are signs of vermin, throw away any food that may be tainted and call in the experts. Don't hesitate. Vermin can spread disease. You don't want them anywhere near your food.

Clean
With everything out, give the pantry itself a thorough clean. Like the fridge, I would start at the top and work down. Wash the outside of the cupboards thoroughly. Hoover the inside, give it a scrub with your preferred cleaning product and then dry thoroughly with a soft cloth. Use that toothbrush to get into any difficult corners. Wipe the jars, tins and bottles with a damp cloth and the cardboard packets with a dry one. Whilst the pantry is airing, you can look to declutter the foodstuffs.

Declutter
Just like the fridge, saving space and preventing waste in the pantry start

when you're shopping. If you want to avoid throwing away too much food, don't buy in larger amounts than you need or your household can reasonably eat. Buying a packet of any foodstuff when you're halfway through the one that you have is a good gauge. It may seem more expensive when you're not succumbing to the sales screams but think about it this way. Do you ever get anything for free? No! For every product that's given away as an offer, the cost of another item you're putting in your basket has been increased to compensate. No supermarket bases its end of year profits on giving away money. So if we don't fall for the offers, even the ones seemingly too good to miss, the supermarkets may well have to change their tactics. They just want to get products off their shelves. Enticing you with these seemingly great offers makes you think 'well I have saved money here, so now I can buy something else'. Remember, the supermarkets pay very clever people a lot of money to find ever more subtle ways of making you part with your hard-earned cash. As I describe elsewhere, shop with a list, get in and get out quick.

When deciding whether to keep or throw away items in your pantry, a good starting place is the dates on the packets, tins, jars and bottles. So let's talk about those pesky little dates. What do the two most important dates actually mean?

According to the United Kingdom Food Standards Agency, these dates mean:

Best Before Date:
This relates to food quality including taste, texture and appearance. Eating food solely past this date is unlikely to be harmful. Cook eggs thoroughly if they're to be eaten one or two days after this date.

Use Before Date:
This is the most important date to consider. This relates to food safety. If you come across food in your pantry that is past its UBD then you should not eat it. There are exceptions to this such as sugar, honey and salt. Freezing food will also extend its shelf life. However, if in doubt do not consume it. I'm not a slave to Best Before or Use Before Dates. I use my best judgement, common sense and experience. This works both ways. Something may be just past its UBD such as honey or salt but in my judgement it's okay to use. However, when it comes to things like meat or fish they can be off even

before their UBD. Today's catch straight off the boat could give you a bout of something nasty if not stored in the correct manner.

Some food may still be safe to eat past its UBD or BBD but may have lost its taste, specifically dry ingredients. Dry yeast may not work after its BBD. I've tried it once. The bread came out like a brick! Chocolate powder may look okay but the flavour will have gone.

The saying about ducks comes to mind. If it walks like a duck, sounds like a duck and looks like a duck, the chances are it's a duck. So, if something smells off, tastes off and looks off, then it's probably off! Throw it away. It's best not to take any chances. Never mind what the label says in this case. Trust your instincts.

Storing food the correct way is vital. Learn about it by reading the label of the foodstuffs you buy until it becomes second nature. Your food will taste better and be healthier for you and your family.

A good declutter of your pantry will improve the quality of both the foodstuffs you use and the meals you prepare.

♥ Tip

Think about transferring foods from their cardboard or plastic packets into airtight glass containers. They look more attractive and last longer. Label them accordingly to prevent mistaking cornflour for icing sugar.

♥ Tip

Whilst you're decluttering the pantry, make a shopping list of things you need to replace.

♥ Tip

Throw away food tins that are rusty or swollen. These are sure signs that all is not well inside! Do not buy dented tins. The tin could be compromised even if only slightly. It doesn't take much for bacteria to get in and start to rot the contents.

Moisture or humidity in the pantry is to be avoided. It can ruin many foods and rot the cardboard of packets. To avoid moisture getting into foods, air the pantry frequently, especially in hot weather and make sure opened packets are properly resealed. Use clothes pegs to ensure paper or plastic packets remain closed or transfer the contents to air tight glass jars. I love glass jars. They make a pretty display and you can see the contents without opening them.

Organise

Have a good think about how you want your pantry organised. Properly done, it can make things easy for you when you're preparing and cooking food. Everything in the pantry needs to be easy to retrieve and well stored. Looking good is the icing on the cake.

Here are a few ways to help you:

Organising the inside with the help of trays, boxes and baskets will make it both practical and attractive.

Grouping things by type (e.g. tinned fruits, tinned vegetables) or by intended use such as baking ingredients or condiments is an organising tip that makes sense. Use baskets or containers for this.

Get stacked shelving so that every single tin is in view, not hidden behind the others.

Add storage space by fixing shelving or hooks on the inside of the doors for small and light items such as spices, kitchen paper and plastic bags.

Store the larger items at the bottom and the smallest at the top.

Painting the inside a light colour will brighten the interior and make the contents look more attractive.

Line the shelves with self-adhesive, washable shelf liners. Choose from an array of attractive designs, colours and finishes.

Once you've finished working on your pantry, give yourself a pat on the back. That was a good job done.

Shelving

Whilst cupboards and drawers are built to keep everything out of sight, shelves display the beautiful or useful. My own shelves are the repository for items that make me feel good. You'll find old china, a cast iron Japanese teapot and pottery made by my sons in primary school. Things that truly only a mother could love, but love them I do and they will always take pride of place in my kitchen. What do you display on your shelves?

Empty
Remove everything from the shelves; that's easy enough.

Clean
Give the shelves a good dusting and cleaning. The items themselves may
need a good wipe as well.

Declutter
Have a good think about what you want to store and display on your shelves.
They will set the mood and tone of your new, tidier kitchen. Displaying too
much makes the shelves look untidy and cluttered. On overcrowded shelves,
nothing seems loved, everything vies for attention and it's a pain to clean.

Organise
Lining your shelves will not only make them easy to clean but also attractive.
Put back only those items that look nice or that you use regularly. Otherwise,
find those things a new home.

Now that you've started decluttering, space will be opening up all around
you. You're rediscovering things that you love and have missed. You're also
finding things that you don't like and can go. Keep only what you love and
use. It makes your kitchen a personal space and one you'll feel more at home
in. More importantly, it'll be a place you'll want to spend more time in.
Every drawer, cupboard and shelf, cleaned and tidied, brings you closer to
your dream kitchen. Go ahead. Change your kitchen and your attitude
towards it.

Sink

The sink is the trusty workhorse of the kitchen. Nothing comes in for more
use and abuse. It's part of the process of every meal, from preparation to
doing the dishes. My mother's sink was always full of food to prepare or
pots, pans and dishes to wash. It was an endless conveyor belt that needed to
be cleared of what was in it so that what needed to go in it could fit! No
wonder the phrase 'being tied to the kitchen sink' is such an apt metaphor for
constant toil.

Empty
Empty the sink...always!

I don't know about you, but nothing makes me grumpier than a sink full of dirty dishes. How can I enjoy my early morning 'café et tartines' with all that mess looking at me? Well, I can't! A messy sink happens to me just as it happens to everyone else; for example after a late dinner party, if I've been unwell or for many other reasons. Bad sinks happen to good people!

A messy sink is like an unmade bed. It's enough to make the whole room look untidy. Once the sink is clean, the whole kitchen appears brighter and cleaner, even if it isn't. So, if there is one task to really knuckle down to, cleaning the sink and keeping it empty and clean is probably my top 'Tidy Kitchen' tip.

Wash all the dishes, dry them and put them away.

Empty the plug drainer into the bin.

Remove everything from the sink and surrounding area. That means sponges, cloths, washing up liquid, scourers and all other things that live there. You should now be able to see your sink in all its glory: empty and ready for a good, thorough clean and scrub.

Clean
Clean your sink with your favourite products, rinse thoroughly and wipe off the excess water. Thoroughly clean the plug, plug hole and garbage disposal if you have one. Pour some bleach or other disinfectant inside them. Wipe the draining board area. Clean the taps and make them shine with some good old elbow grease. Take special care of the nozzle. Clean and disinfect your sponges and cloths, either by soaking them in bleach and water overnight or in the washing machine on a boil wash. Your sink should be sparkling and smell fresh.

Declutter and Organise
Throw away any old sponge or cloth that has seen better days. I prefer to see my sink area clear. If you feel the same, store all your washing up products and utensils under the sink and out of sight. So there shouldn't be much else, if anything at all, to put back on the sink. Try to keep it that way.

♥ Tip
Whilst cooking, fill your sink with hot, soapy water. After you've finished

with a pot, pan, dish or utensil, plunge it in the water immediately. Washing them all later will be easier as the food and grease will already have started to lift off. Even while preparing the rest of the meal, pots and pans in the sink can be washed and put away, when you have a minute or two to spare. A good cook is a tidy cook! Keeping the kitchen clean and tidy as you cook is a great way to save time and effort.

Under The Sink

Isn't it ironic that the area most neglected when it comes to a tidy kitchen, is the one where you keep your cleaning products and tools? After doing the housework you throw them back under the sink, close the door quickly and walk away! But, this area needs to be clean too.

Empty
Remove all the cleaning products and tools. Unclip the bin if you have it attached to the door and take out the bin liner. This is one area where you are bound to find things that don't belong in the kitchen so do keep an empty box handy.

Clean
Under the sink is where the pipes go to the drains, so make sure that there are no leaks and drips whilst you're down there. I know, it's an undignified job but someone has to do it! Wash the interior well, the inside and outside of the door. Wipe dry. Give your pull-out bin a thorough clean too and disinfect it with bleach. A bin doesn't have to be dirty. It needs to be cleaned thoroughly, otherwise it will harbour germs and may attract flies and vermin. Have a happy bin and keep it clean. Give a quick wipe to all your products, I bet they're dusty too.

Declutter
Throw away all empty bottles and anything else that's too grimy to use.

Organise
Those handy shelf liners can be put to good use again to avoid stains and keep the inside looking fresh. Once the cupboard is clean, put everything back in. Look for a tray, bucket or basket to store all your products in, instead of having them loose. It's much easier to pull out one whole container to retrieve a product, rather than groping around in the dark on your hands and

knees.

Walls

Walls, like ceilings, often get forgotten about. However, they get dusty and greasy in a kitchen, just as much as anything else. So, remove all pictures, calendars and all other decorations. Give the walls a good hoovering for any dust and cobwebs. Wash them down with a damp cloth, taking care above and around electric sockets and switches. Use a cleaning product that will be kind to your paint or tiles.

Walls are a great place to display things that make your kitchen a truly personal space. Before hanging them back up on the walls though, give them a good dusting too.

Worktops (Countertops)

Empty
Worktops, along with the sink, are areas that attract anything and everything. They always seem to be covered with things and require constant attention. Today, you need to remove every single object, whether they belong in the kitchen or not.

Clean
Wipe the worktops with the appropriate cleaning product or just a damp, soapy sponge. Clean and disinfect each section. Let it dry well.

Declutter
Go through each item that you removed. Deal with it accordingly. As before, the only things that should remain are those that help you cook in one way or another.

Organise
Try to leave as little as possible on your worktops. As we know, the less you have on show, the easier it is to clean. The best look for worktops is a minimal one. Try to find a place for each item, whether crockery, accessory or appliance, inside your units or drawers.

Conclusion

You should have been writing down the above areas into your 'Declutter Campaign List' in the order you want to tackle them. Your campaign is truly sorted. Now is time for action.

In the next chapter, you will work through your 'Declutter Campaign List' of cleaning jobs one by one. Be flexible and use tasks that can be completed quicker if you're pushed for time. Each completed job will bring you closer to your dream kitchen.

CHAPTER 7
D-Day

Today is D-Day: Declutter Day. You are committed to starting the project right now.

Beginning early in the morning or late at night depends on whether you're a lark or an owl. My own preference is to start as early as possible. As a lark, I live by the motto 'The earlier I start the earlier I finish'. If you're an owl though, please be careful not to disturb the neighbours with late night cleaning.

If you only have one hour, you can make a dent in the project. The key is to do something, however small, regularly. Actions bring results.

Put on an apron or clothes you don't mind getting dirty, especially if you're going to be cleaning and degreasing any areas.

Get all your cleaning products ready, whether natural or not: white vinegar, lemon halves, baking soda, bleach, all-purpose cleaner, glass spray, wood polisher, antibacterial wipes, kitchen cleaner spray, scouring powder or anything else you usually clean with.

CAUTION: Never mix cleaning products together, use separately. Always read and follow the label before using.

Bring out the cleaning tools adequate for the tasks: sponges, newspaper, cloths, rags, feather duster, hoover, broom, brush, mop, bucket of hot soapy water, scourers, kitchen towels, toothpicks, cotton buds and any other tools you need.

Place four empty boxes on the floor, labelled 'handovers, give-aways, sells, and throw-outs'. They will get filled with items belonging to each member of the family, to give away to charity or friends, to be sold or thrown out. You could also have an extra box labelled 'Unsure', as described above.

Bring the rubbish bin close to where you'll be working, into which you'll throw all expired foodstuffs you find.

Have plenty of water to drink close at hand.

Put on some good lively music to get your heart pumping and your rhythm going.

If the weather's nice, throw open the windows to let the light and fresh air in. The more oxygen you have available, the better you'll feel during the task. Believe me, when you're cleaning vigourously you build up a good healthy glow.

Now Start!

Whatever you've chosen to do, just begin. No dithering, no second guessing.

Get out your 'Declutter Campaign List' and decide on your first task or tasks.

Go through the four step program (Empty, Clean, Declutter and Organise) for each task.

Repeat this with every task until all the tasks are crossed off your 'Declutter Campaign List'.

Whether this takes a day, week or month, it doesn't matter. When you cross off the final task, congratulations, you are the proud owner of a tidy and organised kitchen.

Time for that reward!

Head down to Chapter 8 for more ideas on organisation.

CHAPTER 8
Organisation

All Kitchens Great and Small

Some people have compact but perfectly formed kitchens. Others have large and well equipped ones. Whichever you have, I hold the belief that space in a kitchen should work for you. When clutter and disorganisation take over, you work for the space. As a consequence, it's harder to find room. You have to move things around, push them about or stack them on top of each other before you can do any cooking. This doesn't save space or time: it wastes both. However, even just a little organisation can improve the situation remarkably and remove mounting frustration.

All kitchens great and small can suffer from a lack of organisation. Compare, 'my kitchen is so small there is no room to store anything, that's why it's cluttered' to 'my kitchen is so large I can keep everything and anything on display, that's why it's cluttered'.

Truly, size doesn't matter. It's organisation or the lack of it that counts. Let's look at a few issues and try to find solutions for them.

Busy Open Shelves

I have mentioned shelves already, but I want to explore them in more detail. Open shelves are those in full view and not enclosed in a cupboard or behind any kind of door. Shelving is a necessity; especially in small kitchens. It allows things to be accessed quickly and easily. So, what's on it should be something that's used often or is attractive.

Busy shelves can make even the tidiest kitchen look cluttered, so just think what they do to an already cluttered one.

Solution

Think long and hard about the purpose of open shelving in your kitchen.

Is it just to display things that have no other place or purpose? If so, re-think their role in the kitchen as previously discussed.
Is it to use as storage which is scarce? If so, tidy up and make the display easy on the eye too, not just practical.
If displaying cookery books, arrange them according to size. Give some thought to order.

Stand back and look at the reorganised shelves. Make changes as necessary. Even the utilitarian can be made to look attractive.

Decant ingredients from their ordinary packets into chic containers. They serve a function and look pretty as well.

Want to display things such as tea pots, water jugs or plates? Odd numbers are more appealing than even numbers so group them together in threes or fives. If you have numerous teapots, remember that you don't have to show them all at once. Choose and display only your favourites. Put the others away and rotate them out every now and then.

If displaying glass jars, ensure that they're clean, not grubby and greasy. Sort them by size, type and/or colour of contents. Look online for collections of similar objects and ideas for displays. Choose an arrangement that looks good but is also practical.

Think of your shelves almost like a work of art. Spend time over them as they will be on show 24/7.

Baskets, Boxes, Containers and Jars

Anybody who enjoys organising will vouch for the usefulness and necessity of boxes and containers of varying sizes. They can be used in drawers, inside units, on shelving, even inside the fridge or freezer. They make any space look instantly tidy and organised. They help in cleaning, as the boxes, along with the contents, are much easier to move than all the items individually. Invest in them or look around your home. You may find some old perfume or gift boxes that can do the job well. Many of them are pretty and can serve to store small baking supplies, for instance.

In my kitchen, I use wicker baskets inside my units. I store jars and packets in them. If I need anything, I take out the whole basket and look for what I need. This is easier than standing on tip toe, rummaging at the back of a cupboard, moving things around, knocking them over, spilling stuff and getting frustrated. The added advantage of baskets is that I can use all the available space, even right to the back of the units without fear of never being able to reach anything.

Baskets are attractive and practical. When I open my cupboard doors, all I see are nice baskets, not an odd assortment of packets, jars and culinary mayhem. Everything looks much neater.

Use baskets, boxes, containers and jars for whatever you want. Try to keep the design of the boxes simple and to one or two styles to keep them visually tidy. Any boxes can assist with the immediate problem. The more homogenous and simple the design, the less cluttered your kitchen will feel. You can always decorate them with attractive wrapping paper so they match. Too many competing styles can appear just as cluttered as what you're trying to keep tidy. However, if you like the eclectic style and want different designs and types of boxes, then go for it. Please send me photos, I would love to see your own organising solutions.

Spices look more appealing in glass jars than sitting in opened plastic wrappers, cardboard or paper packets.

You can use containers in the fridge too. Give your 'fromages' a French look by keeping them in a wicker or wooden box lined with gingham. Sachets of this and that can be kept together in plastic containers. Small bottles of this, that and the other can be put in those little brown paper bags that you get your lunch in from sandwich shops (just make sure they're strong enough and don't split!).

Storage Concepts

Corner units can be a problem. Reaching things at the back is awkward. I've seen some kitchens where these areas were boxed in just because they would have been too deep. What a waste of space! Luckily, kitchen design has moved on. Carousels can be fitted into corner units in order to use all available space.

Pull-out pantry drawers and units also offer the same concept. They make all space usable. If you're having your kitchen remodelled, a good designer can make much more room available than you thought possible.

Deep drawers under the hob are so practical for storing large and heavy pots and pans or electrical appliances such as food processors, bread makers and mixers. There's no need to bend down to move heavy items out of the way to get at what you want. Remember, the more awkward it is to get something out, the less likely it will be used. Good kitchen design cuts down on heavy lifting and means less backache!

If you're currently planning a new kitchen, talk to the designer. There's no need to think that a properly planned kitchen is out of your price range. In most stores, even DIY, the kitchen design is a free service. Think about all aspects of your kitchen. Redesigning is the ideal opportunity to plan for how you'd like to use your kitchen. If you want to do more baking, design it with that in mind. Once it's in the design, you are more likely to do it.

♥ Tip

When planning your kitchen, think carefully about lighting. Worktops under wall units can be dark, so look at under-unit lighting. Be careful though. These lights can get hot, so watch what you keep in the units above them. Your secret chocolate stash can soon melt and become unappealing.

Close To You

Keep everything in your kitchen close to where you're going to use it. This will save time when preparing and cooking meals.

For example, keep salt and pepper next to the hob. Keep coffee, tea and sugar next to the kettle. This may sound obvious to many of you but some people walk up and down their kitchen several times just to make a cup of tea. When I witness this, I can feel my fingers itching to pick up their cups, tea and sugar and place them in the cupboard next to their kettle.

A heavy stand mixer, food processor or bread machine should be close to where you prepare food or bake. If used a lot, by all means keep them on the worktop, as they're heavy to lift. I have my own stand mixer on the worktop, ready to go at a moment's notice or inspiration.

The Triangle Of Work

Many cooks don't know about this simple but important ergonomic principle.

Cooker, sink and fridge are the three points of your triangle of work. You shouldn't have to walk far from any of them to the other two. The path and worktops between them should be clear and unobstructed. If you think about it, you'll see the logic and simplicity. If any is too far from the others, you'll spend more time walking than cooking.

If the cooker is too far from the sink, heavy pots and pans, filled with boiling water, need carrying a long way. That's dangerous, so the shorter the trip the better.
If the fridge is too far from the sink or cooker, you have to walk some distance to carry ingredients to where they'll be washed, prepared or cooked.

Even a galley kitchen, with its long, narrow layout, can be improved by simply having as short a distance between these three areas as possible, rather than at opposite ends of the worktop.

When designing your kitchen, think long and hard about this triangle.

Practicality

The way you work, the ingredients you use regularly and the design of your kitchen determine where things will go in your units, drawers or on shelves. The confines of this book don't allow the space to advise on every single aspect but general principles apply to all kitchens.

Think practically about pots, pans, foodstuffs, china and utensils. The things you can't cook without should be next to the hob and/or oven.

If you don't want to keep salt, pepper and cooking oils on the worktop, store them inside the closest cupboard. Make sure they can be brought out easily by placing them all in one basket.

The pantry should be as close to the triangle of work as possible but far enough away so that the packet and dried goods don't get affected by steam and heat from the kitchen.

Bottles of wine may look attractive in a tower down the side of the oven but the heat will make the wine go off. Wine should be kept cool and calm, away from the hustle and bustle of the kitchen. However, keeping a couple of bottles of white wine or Champagne in the fridge is a great idea for any impromptu soirée.

Group condiments together in the fridge or in a cupboard (pantry), close to where you need them most.

Vegetables can be kept in the crisper in the fridge. Alternatively, if your kitchen never gets too hot, display them in a basket or vegetable rack, close to the sink.

Eggs can be kept in the fridge. I keep mine on display on my worktop, out of direct sunlight and heat, which can make them go off quickly.

♥ Tip

If you remove eggs from their box to display in a basket or if you put them in the fridge door, do make a note of their 'use by' date, or you may cook with eggs that are too old. Write the date on the shell or on a note tucked into the basket.

♥ Tip

If you regularly bake the same things, store the dry ingredients and the utensils you need inside the mixing bowl. Keep this in a cool place next to where you mix your dough or pastry. Everything is then ready to go and to hand in one place! You can even keep some eggs, butter and milk in the same container in the fridge ready to go. Only two trips and you're set to bake.

These are only a few examples of how you can make sense of your everyday kitchen and meal time needs. Doubtless, what works for me may not work for you. Do let me know your solutions as I'm sure you can think of things that I haven't thought of. I love to hear from readers and learn new things.

Aesthetics

The kitchen may be the last place you'd think could benefit from aesthetics. Can it look pretty too? 'Bien sûr'! A kitchen has to be functional as it's a working area. Utility doesn't have to be separate from beauty. There is a beauty in good function. Consider my other love, clothes! They are utilitarian but have spawned a multi-billion pound industry based on aesthetics. The same can be said about the kitchen. See it through new eyes. Simple things are the best, as always, in everything. No need to rip out your whole kitchen. A few small changes can make an impact. Clear your table and add a small 'chemin de table' with a bunch of flowers or basket of fresh fruit. Leave a wooden table bare to look fresh and inviting. Instant kitchen chic.

Match utensils if they're kept on display. If you have stainless steel appliances, go for stainless steel utensils. Try for uniformity of style. This helps make the kitchen look tidy and organised.

Keep worktops clear. Yes, every day.

Keep cleaning products out of sight under the sink, where they belong.

Avoid fancy curtains on kitchen windows. They attract dust and grease. Hang simple blinds that can be wiped clean or nothing at all.

Keep all displays harmonious.

Fold your tea or hand towels neatly, don't just throw them on the worktops.

In conclusion, make everything in the kitchen work for the space it occupies.

CHAPTER 9
Keep It All Going

You motivated yourself to tidy and organise your kitchen. You found the time you needed, whether by chunking or sweating it out, bravo! You worked hard and it shows.

Step back and admire your handy work. The worktops are clear, the sink is gleaming. Nothing is out of place. Everything has a purpose and a function. It's a kitchen to be proud of. I bet you just can't wait to show it off. Tweet it out or post it on your Facebook page so that we can all share in your pride. Write your final blog entry. Do you feel like baking a scrumptious batch of cookies? Go ahead. This is what your kitchen is for. Don't forget to collect on that reward you promised yourself.

After the hard work it took to get the kitchen back into shape, keeping the momentum going is essential. It can soon slide back into the state it was before. By its very nature, a kitchen will get messy and take a daily battering. One minute it's perfect, then, in the time it takes to bake a cake, it looks like a flour bomb has gone off. It's mayhem again. Did you make this effort for nothing? Of course not. Read on for a few ways to ensure that the kitchen never looks far off its best.

Tidy and wipe as you go. Ideally, you should wash, dry and put away all dishes, cutlery, pots and pans after use. If this is really impossible, at the very least, place them into the sink or dishwasher. Even if either gets to overflowing, at least those dishes will be in one place and the worktops will be clear.

When in a hurry, don't peel potatoes or other vegetables into the sink. It's time consuming to clear up after. Instead, place the bin at your feet during peeling so that the scraps can drop into the bin as you peel.

When cooking, put eggs, butter and any condiments straight back into the fridge after use. It literally takes seconds. Don't let anything build up on the worktops unnecessarily.

Put every item from your daily and weekly shop in its place straight away. My own way of doing it is as follows. Would you believe that keeping my kitchen tidy and organised starts at the till? When I pack my groceries, I ensure that everything is grouped into different bags destined for separate areas: frozen foods, fruit and vegetables, pantry goods, cleaning and all other products. When I get home, I place the bag of cleaning products next to the sink. The bag of pantry food I leave on the worktop next to the pantry. I then head for the fridge/freezer with the cool food. I empty these straight in so that they don't stand around in the warmth. I then pack away the rest in their appropriate places. When all items for the kitchen have been stored away, anything remaining, such as toiletries, are taken straight to where they belong. This avoids all the troublesome unpacking and zigzagging around the kitchen for ten minutes.

When finished, fold your reusable shopping bags. Tidy these away too, either in your car, drawer or shopping trolley.

Before placing wrapped foods in the fridge, remove the outer packaging. It'll be much easier, later on, to take out one yoghurt instead of the whole pack. No more torn wrappers in the fridge, 'Merci'! The fridge will look tidier for it.

Unwrap and stack snacks inside a tray or box in the fridge.

Remove vegetables from their plastic wrappers and place them inside the crisper in the fridge. They won't sweat and thus will last longer. The proper storing of vegetables is a book in itself!

After any meal, clear up the table, sink and worktops. Give all surfaces one final wipe and you're done.

Lists

As mentioned earlier in the book, lists should not be written just before heading out to the shops. That's too late. You'll miss things. The correct way to make a shopping list is to write it as and when you realise you need something. This may be days before you go to the shops but it'll ensure that the list is continually updated. If you pass a shop and buy something you need, cross it off. A last minute list is a bad list. Keep a pad in a prominent place in the kitchen. It doesn't get more basic than that. As you prepare, cook, wipe or clean, you'll notice things that you need to buy. Write them down straight away. Don't leave it to chance or think you'll remember. The odds are you won't. Did I use the flour or not? Do I need more butter? Did I use all the eggs? Left to memory, you will second guess yourself. Writing down what you need will ensure you buy the things in the right amounts at the right time. Stick to your lists and don't overbuy. Write down any utensil, gadget or appliance that you need desperately. Sticking to your list will save you money, prevents wastage, diminishes clutter and makes your kitchen work for you. Try it, you may get hooked on lists!

♥ Tip

Take a pen on your shopping trip and cross out each item once it's in your trolley. This isn't as daft or obvious as it may sound. It ensures that you won't forget anything or miss it amongst all the other items. It serves as a most important trigger. Once all items are crossed off, head directly to the check out, do not saunter or graze.

Mind Games

Supermarkets lead us through their shops in the order they want us to go. As it isn't always the most logical route, who says you have to follow that?

Frozen foods, for instance, are usually found in the middle of the store. If you follow its layout, you'll be at the frozen products way before you finish your shopping. So, if you prefer your ice cream or pizza to remain frozen, go to this section last.

If you want to save time and money, follow your list to the letter. Supermarkets have the annoying habit of moving displays. This is a ploy to make you look for things and keep you inside the shop for as long as possible. A disoriented shopper is more susceptible to psychological advertising than one who knows what she wants and where to get it. Don't be a grazer! Grazing is when you shop aimlessly, looking at everything and anything without a plan. Be a predator instead. Walk quickly and smartly. Focus on your list, not the adverts, slogans and offers. This way, you will not overbuy.

♥ Tip

To ensure frozen food does not defrost before you get home, pack it directly into chill bags at the till or into a cool box in the car. Frozen products that have defrosted should not be refrozen.

Sales

I love the sales just like anyone else. Saving while spending gives us a high, 'Non'? But sticking only to what we need can be difficult. However, this is the way to avoid filling up our homes with more clutter. Again, even in the sales, take a list and stick to it. Try too see things as needs, not wants. Do I need a new kettle or do I want it? Do I need the latest mixing-juicing-breadmaking-all-in-one-slicing-dicing-peeling-coring electric thingy or do I merely want it? It's easy to get carried along in the frenzy of the sales. By the time you get home, you're already beginning to wonder how it all happened.

Here are some tips on how to resist the lure of the sales:

Avoid going at all.
Don't go on the first day. The feeding frenzy really is too much to resist.
Don't buy anything on the first day. Go back the next day.
Follow your list and do not deviate.
Take only enough cash for what you need.
Go along with no money at all to see what's on offer.
Bring a money-minded friend who will tut tut every time you pick something up.
Take a friend who needs to do the same as you. Encourage each other not to overspend.
Take your husband with you. That always puts the chill on sales fever!
Give your list to a partner or friend. They're in charge of it and will steer you toward what you need. They mustn't allow you to buy items not on the list.
Swap lists of items you need with a friend and give each other only sufficient cash for those items. They buy what you need and vice versa. You won't want to spend someone else's money!

Daily Regime

We're all human. We get overwhelmed at times. When we let things slip, they get unmanageable soon enough. There's no alternative but to bite the bullet and start again. It might take a couple of hours and then it's done. Try to get the habit of tidying and cleaning up every day. When you have some spare time, declutter one unit or area. Get rid of opened packets of uneaten or old food. Throw away a chipped plate, the buckled frying pan, the leaky jug and the empty jars meant for making jam you never will. There's a Zen saying which goes 'if you see a weed, pick it up'. This simply means, keep on top of things.

The following is the minimum that needs to be done to keep your kitchen ticking over:

Clear the table after every use.
Wash dishes straight away or stack them in the dishwasher.
Remove anything that doesn't belong in the kitchen.
Sweep the kitchen floor.
Fold up dish cloths.
Empty the bin.
Clean the sink.

Give your oven and hob a quick wipe after each use. Remove any baked-on spills as well as you can. Once a fortnight or depending on use, clean your oven thoroughly.

Wipe spills in the microwave straight away. It only takes seconds when the spill is fresh. It may take forever if you leave it.

Wipe worktops at least once a day and preferably after every use. You should really wipe them down before use as well, as flies or the cat may have wandered across.

When wiping worktops, lift the microwave, toaster and kettle in order to reach underneath. Don't fall into the trap of wiping around things and considering that the job is done.

All the above can be done quickly and easily. They prevent the kitchen from descending into chaos.

Working From Home

When you work from home, it can be difficult to keep things spick and span on a daily basis. You think you can do the cleaning and tidying up later. However, as you get engrossed with your work, the 'later' never comes and the mess piles up. As a writer, I've found a way that works for me. I give myself little breaks throughout the day, breaking off from my computer every half hour for five minutes or every hour for fifteen. During these short breaks, I can do plenty. As well as straightening up the rest of the house, I can keep on top of things in the kitchen.

During the five minute breaks, you have enough time to do any of these tasks:

Clear the breakfast dishes from the table.
Wipe the table and add a vase of flowers or fruit basket.
Fill the dishwasher and turn it on or
Wash the dishes (from breakfast) under the running tap to save time.
Dry the dishes and put them away.
Wipe all the worktops with a soapy sponge or antibacterial wipe.
Clean the kitchen window, window sill, wipe the blind.
Wipe the interior of the microwave.

In a quarter of an hour, you can do any of the following:

Wash, dry and put dishes away, clean your sink, make it sparkle.
Hoover the kitchen.
Wash the floor.
Empty the fridge, don't remove the shelves but wipe them with a wet cloth or sponge, put food back inside tidily.
Clean and buff up the front of all your large appliances.

Put an egg-timer on during every break. It helps enormously. Try to hurry up during each task. You'll feel energised and look forward to the next one. These physical breaks are great intervals from mind work. You may find that you achieve more.

For stay-at-home mums, organisation is still important. The five and fifteen minute breaks can be done in between looking after the children and all the many other jobs you have to do. The key is a little and often, which will keep you on top of all the tasks.

Helping Hands

We have busier lives now than we ever did. Our days are crammed with all sorts of activities, work, social events, children, sports, hobbies, housework and travelling. Even our days off are filled to bursting with all the things we want to do during the working week but haven't got time for. It's natural to get overwhelmed by the amount of time it takes to tidy, declutter and organise your kitchen. After a hard day's work, the last ounce of energy you have after dinner is used to haul yourself to the bathroom to get ready for bed. The dishes, sink and hob can wait. Do you feel like this most nights? I've been there, so have many other women. Research has shown that it's women who do the bulk of the household chores, 'Quelle surprise'!

If clearing up after a meal you've shopped for, prepared, cooked and served seems like the last straw, who could blame you? Many of us prefer to do the task ourselves as the job will get done faster. We also avoid the battle that always comes if we ask for help. However, never asking can create a rod for your own back. Your partner will get used to putting his feet under the table and then up in front of the TV whilst you dart about doing all the work. This may create arguments and resentment that can grow and fester for years. Sharing a good meal around the table and clearing up together afterwards make a family bond more. Your partner and children will learn to contribute to the housework and hopefully come to appreciate what you do.

Learn to ask for help. It may be too much hard work to drag children away from computer games and social networks but this is part of their education too. Yes, there will be moans and gripes at first, but give it a chance. Make it fun with younger children. Turn it into a game or by offering them treats and rewards. With your partner, well, try offering treats and rewards! A job that takes you 30 minutes to do by yourself can take a fraction of that when you all pitch in together.

For example, if you're washing the dishes by yourself, suggest that you need to talk to one member of the family. While at the sink together, chat about anything. By the time the dishes are done, you've had a conversation and they've been roped into helping without realising it.

There will be resistance of course and many, many excuses, but stay strong. If it comes to it, insist. The next day, do it again. Eventually, help may arrive unrequested. Dare to dream…

Keep asking for help. There's nothing to lose! Find ways to entice people to provide assistance. Whatever you do, try to take the 'Hel' out of Help. You may be surprised by the result.

To prove to your family that cleaning the kitchen takes only minutes, try the following steps:

Before getting up from the table, ask them to pass their plates and cutlery down to you. You can stack the plates with the cutlery on top. Even this can save time.

Next, ask each person to pick up something from the table and put it away. If one person takes the salt and pepper, another takes the mustard, again you're left with less to do.

Whilst you take the plates to the sink (or you can ask someone else to do it), get one person to wipe down the table, and another to push in the chairs.

You may change the above to suit your routine but you get the point. You don't even have to do it all on one day. If you're starting from a position where nobody helps at all, for one week just ask people to pass all the plates down to you. The next week, ask for the plates and ask each one to put something away. Gradually, ramp up the ante. Everyone will get used to helping, instead of leaving it all to you. Ask, ask, ask!

If you think this is impossible or won't work in your house, why don't you try?

When To Do The Big Decluttering Purges

The kitchen is different to the other rooms in the house. Going through your units, appliances and fridge is a necessity. Kitchen hygiene has a vital role to play in the health and well-being of you and your family. A messy kitchen may put your health at risk. Food that's gone bad can provide a home for vermin! The kitchen is the area of your home where you have to be the most careful and conscientious.

Regular decluttering and cleaning are necessary routines to add to your busy schedule. This will keep your food and food preparation areas in a proper state. If you really can't face the thought of deep cleaning your kitchen even once a month, make sure that you keep on top of the daily chores given above. This will give you less to do in one go. You can use the natural seasons to provide reminders to do more thorough cleans. There is always something to be done in the kitchen and the seasons can provide ideal opportunities for rearranging and cleaning to suit.

Deep cleaning a dirty and messy kitchen may take up to two full days, if you work by yourself. It's a really big task, but one which has to be done.

Once a fortnight, clean the front and side of the units, cupboards and drawers.

Once a month, wipe clean the top of wall units and replace the newspaper if you're using that earlier tip.

By cleaning in rotation, the majority of your kitchen will always be clean and clutter free. Try to clean your fridge every week before a big shop to provide clean shelves and drawers for new food. As mentioned earlier, it also serves as an opportunity to write your shopping list.

I sincerely hope that, once you've tidied and organised your kitchen, you'll never have to repeat the full regime. If you do, you know that I'll be here to help you.

In addition to the practical aspects of keeping it all going given above, here are some psychological or emotional factors for you to consider.

Use Your Best

Have you ever thought about using your best china every day? Why not? Feel that you deserve to do so, not just on special occasions.

Some people use cheap, cracked and chipped dishes every day. The funny thing is that they may own fabulous china that's only kept for best. I used to be like this, preferring to leave my wedding china for entertaining only. I used it a few times a year. What a shame. Eventually, I realised that life is too short and my family too precious to serve their meals on ordinary, chipped plates. Here's the thing. Every meal is a chance to entertain. Why wait for guests? You and yours deserve the best, three meals a day, 365 days of the year. If you think about it, that's over 1,000 meals. If your best goes unused, it amounts to 1,000 missed opportunities. If you owned a beautiful painting, would you lock it away or would you hang it where you could see it?

The worry of breakages may be stopping you from using your best things. Let me tell you a little story. My husband, who's a keen martial artist, went to Japan to study under a famous teacher. The group he travelled with were invited for tea at a Buddhist temple. The priest served them tea in 1,000 year-old cups. One student asked the priest if he was worried the cups would get broken. He replied "I am ninety and do not worry that hard practice will make me ill". The meaning was quite clear. The cup is a cup. If it gets damaged, that's its destiny. So, use your precious china. Of course, do be careful. The priest showed each student how to handle the cups to lower the risk of damage. In using something precious, don't be blasé, treat it well and honour it.

Acknowledge that every day is special. Use your best china. Eat quality food, drink your fine wines. You are special. Make every day extraordinary, not ordinary. It will make a difference to how you and your family feel. Enjoy!

Appreciation

Nowadays, we're better off financially than previous generations, can afford expensive appliances and all the mod cons. Most of us don't have to save up for years to buy what we want. Instead, we whip out the credit card and head off to the shops. In addition, shopping online removes the inconvenience of leaving the home. The result is that there's no sense of achievement in buying anything. Achievement has been replaced by a never ending sense of entitlement. It doesn't feel like we've spent any money, time or effort to get what we want. As a consequence, there is no appreciation for what we have. In the old days, when you had to save up for something, it took some time to do so. This served as an enforced cooling-off period. When you finally had the cash to spend, you'd had the opportunity to think long and hard about whether or not it was worth it. You also had to go to the shop to buy it and carry it home yourself! Now things appear in your home or on your doorstep as if by magic. No time, no effort, no thought = no appreciation. We feel that things are easily replaceable. They don't deserve our consideration. I no longer take things for granted and practice appreciation every day now. Try it yourself.

Try to slow down. Stop and stare at things, yes, even ordinary, humble things. Fill your life with wonder and appreciation.

CONCLUSION

Bravo! Your kitchen is now tidied and organised, exactly as you set out to do.

What a journey you've had. We concluded that you were most likely to be a clutterer not a hoarder and we examined the excuses you resorted to for not getting the job done. We considered the situation you were in and decided that you lacked the know-how and motivation necessary. We also discussed the ways that clutter affected your life and showed you the benefits of a tidy kitchen. I gave you tools to motivate yourself along the way to achieving the kitchen you longed for but couldn't attain.

I gave you the four-step plan on how to tidy and organise the kitchen to get you started and detailed each area of the kitchen to be tackled. There was a chapter on ways to organise your kitchen to make it a practical place to cook in. Most importantly, you set out your 'Declutter Campaign' and followed it to success.

Along with advice, ideas and tips, this book gave you exercises to make you a thoughtful participant on your quest. The things you found out about your kitchen and yourself will hold you in good stead.

Well, you have turned it all around. You've cracked it. I was with you along the way, encouraging and helping you.

I sincerely hope that you've enjoyed reading The Tidy Kitchen and that it's given you the inspiration, motivation and tools necessary. Sometimes things may slip. Bad kitchens, just like bad sinks, happen to good people. Don't lose heart. I will still be here for you.

Final Exercise

Honest reviews are the silent applause for authors. Please take just a few moments out of your hectic schedule, whilst sitting at your kitchen table enjoying your coffee and croissant perhaps, to practice your appreciation for this book by leaving an honest review on Amazon, 'Merci',

'A bientôt'